Color by Numbers

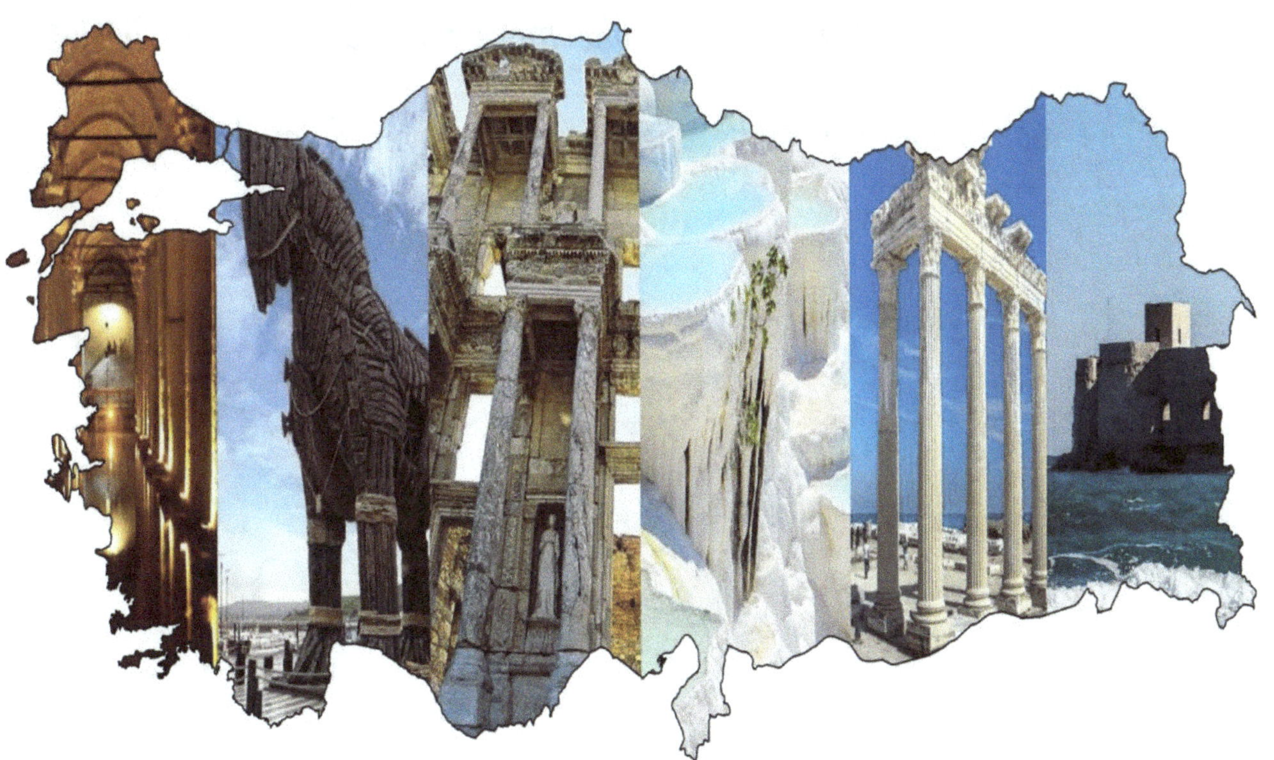

Türkiye

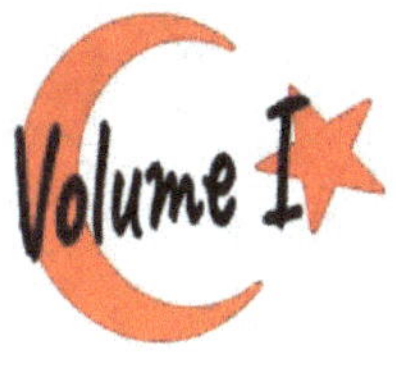

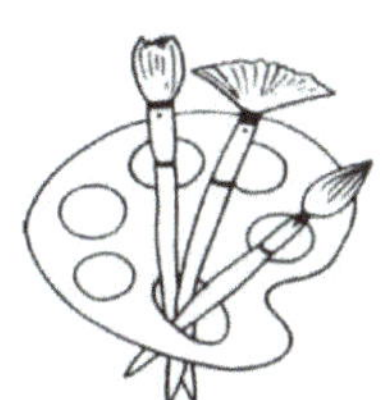

A Tailored Image Studio *by Stacy Bledsoe*

Buisness Card

Map of Türkiye

In this book you will be covering the more polpular sites in Türkiye.

The map below highlights the provinces covered in this book.

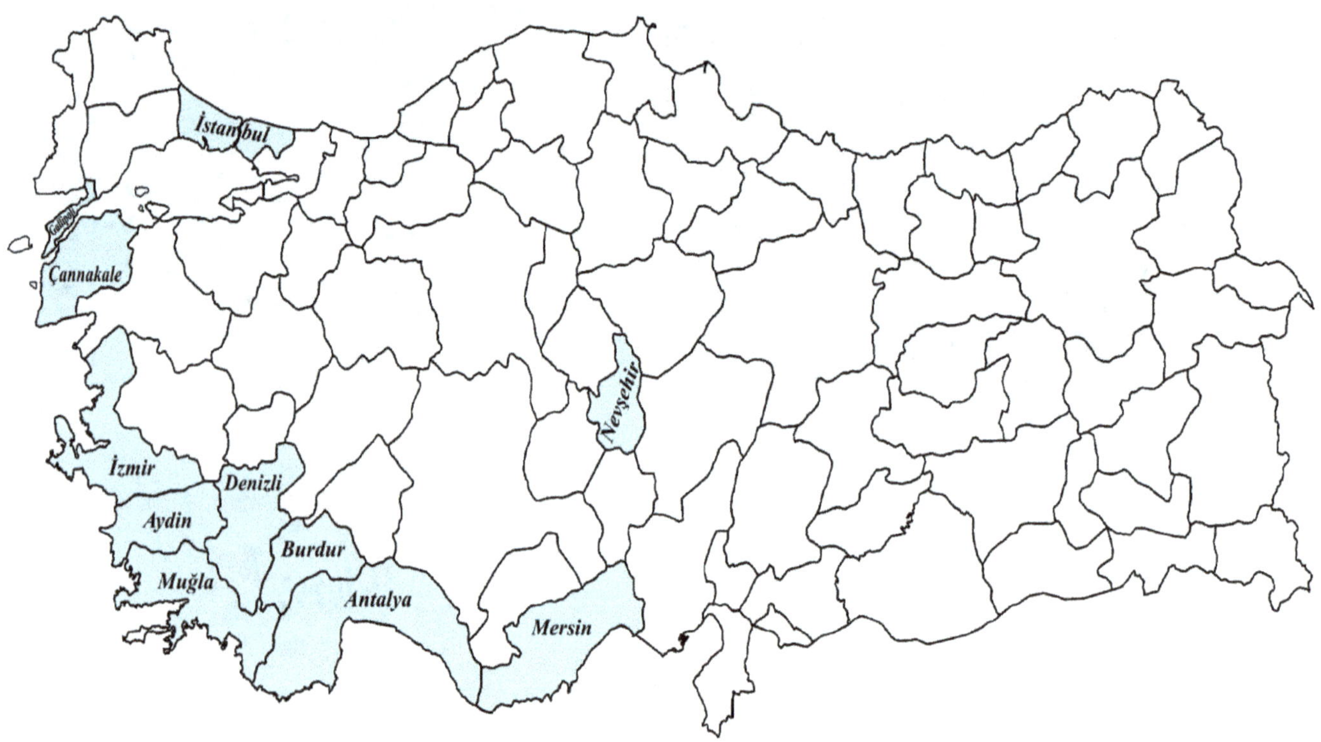

Enjoy your journey!

Tips and help page

- *Color by numbers can be tricky and confusing at times. Not all of the shapes have a number. Sometimes the numbers are hard to find. Sometimes the lines look like a jumbled mess.*

- *Each design piece has a unique QR code that can be scanned with an electronic device (such as a smartphone or tablet). Scanning the code will give you a link to a file. Click on the link, (you may need to approve the download). These files (35 in total) are a breakdown of every color in each design's color palette.*

- *Each design piece has a unique color palette and test swatch area. Use the test swatch area to try and match the colors on the color palettes.*

- *Each color on the unique color palette has an assigned number. Every shape with that number on the design page will be filled in with that color. For example, the number 3 on the color palette is blue. Fill in every shape that has the number 3 with that color of blue. Continue this process for every color on the color palette.*

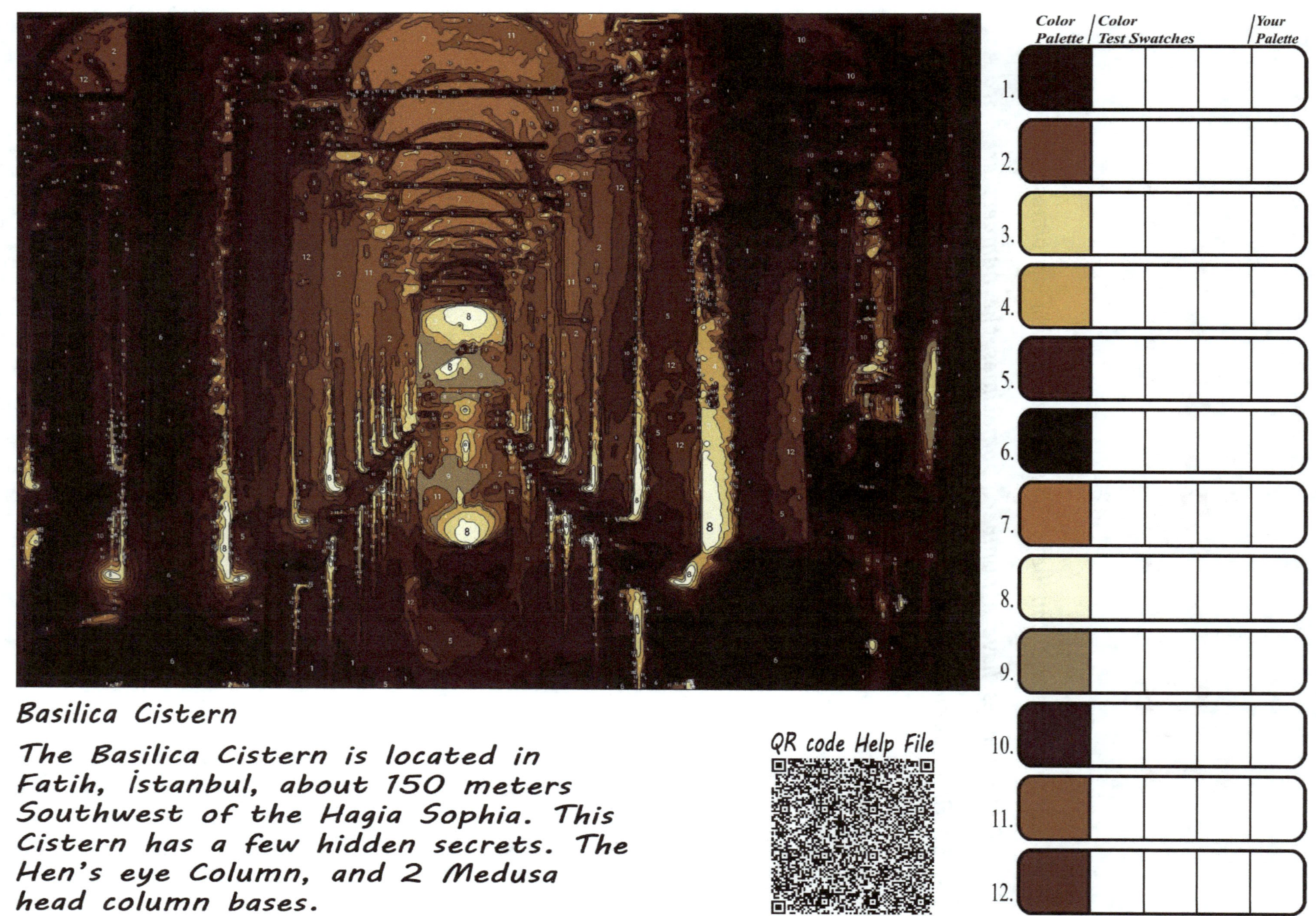

Basilica Cistern

The Basilica Cistern is located in Fatih, İstanbul, about 150 meters Southwest of the Hagia Sophia. This Cistern has a few hidden secrets. The Hen's eye Column, and 2 Medusa head column bases.

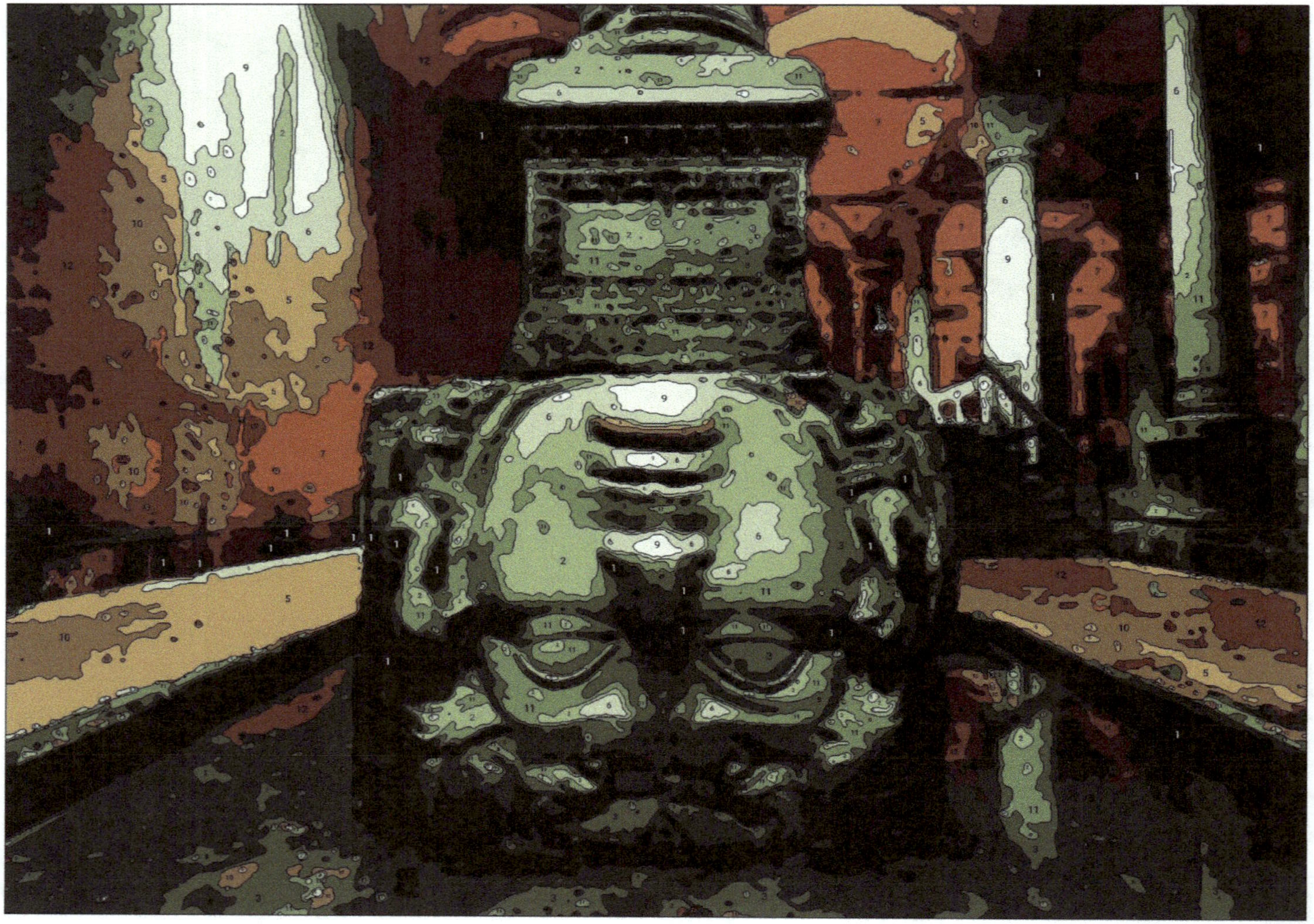

	Color Palette	Color Test Swatches				Your Palette
1.						
2.						
3.						
4.						
5.						
6.						
7.						
8.						
9.						
10.						
11.						
12.						

Medusa's Head Pillar Base

There are two Medusa's head pillar bases in the Basilica Cistern in Fatih, İstanbul. One of the heads is upside down, the other is lying on its side. It is thought that Medusa could not turn you into stone with her head in these positions. It is not known when these heads were placed in the Basilica Cistern, and who placed them there, or why is also unknown.

QR code Help File

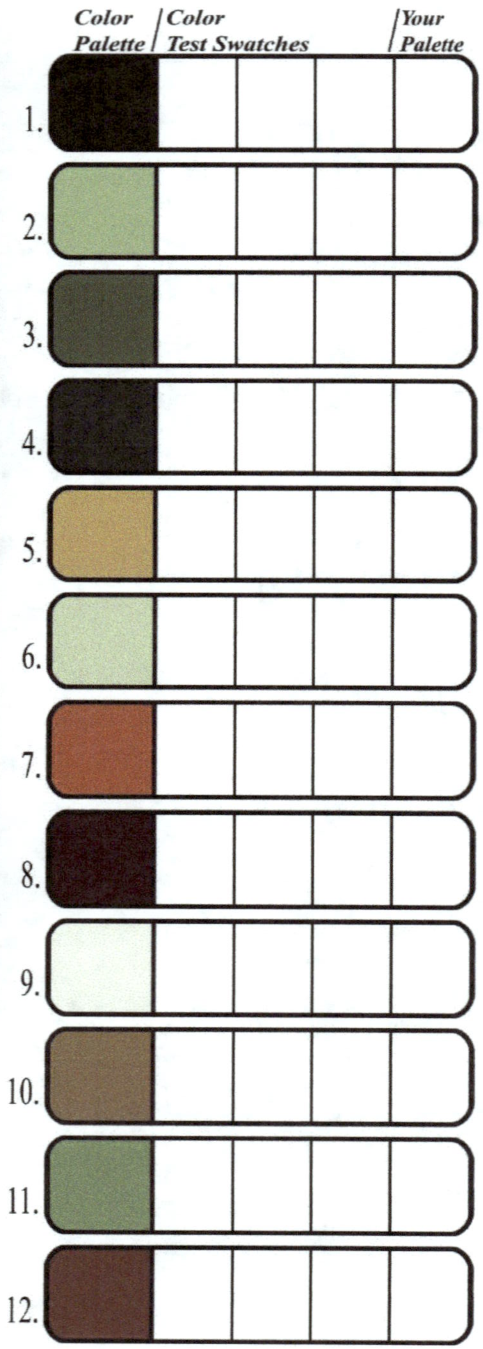

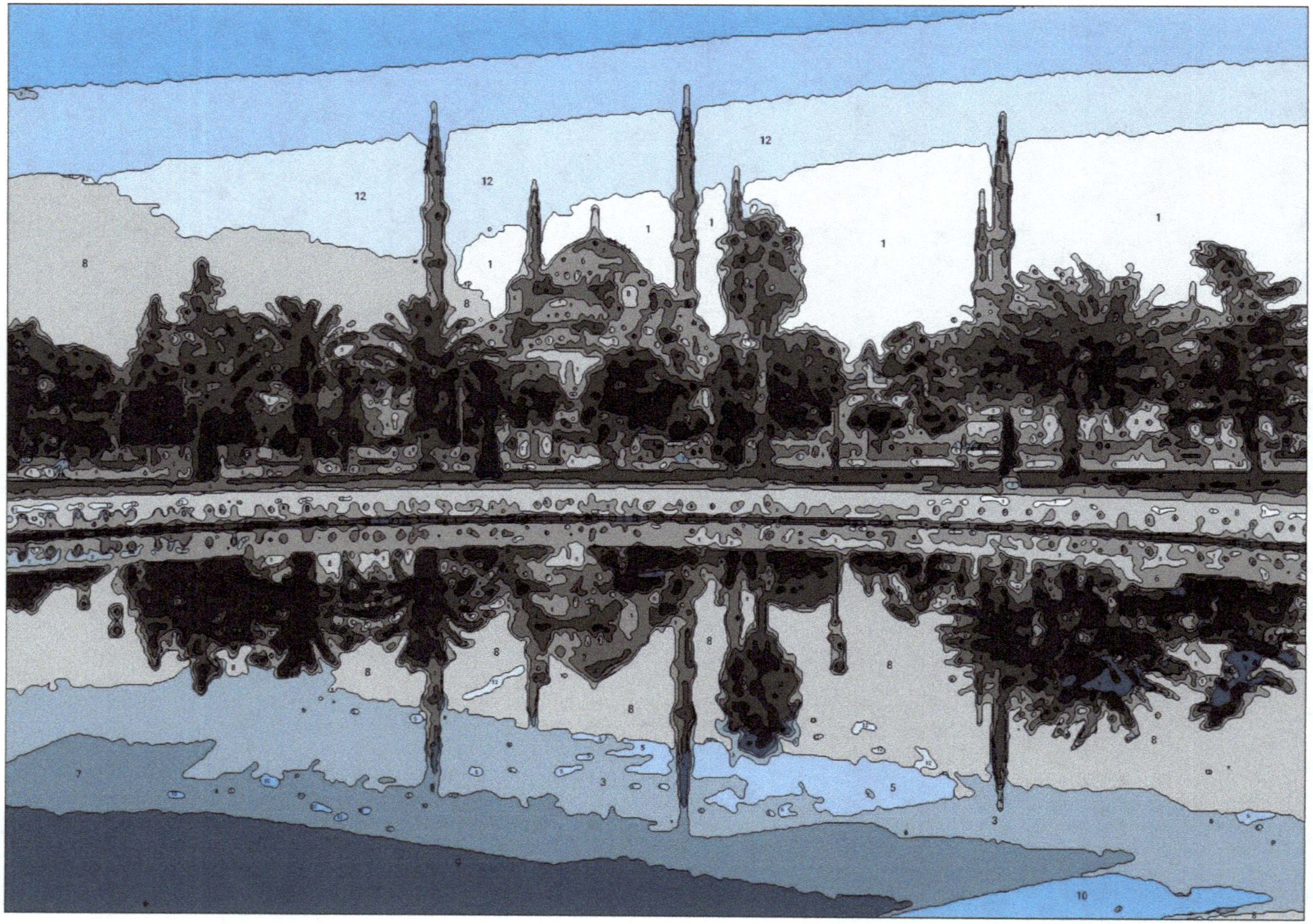

	Color Palette	Color Test Swatches			Your Palette
1.					
2.					
3.					
4.					
5.					
6.					
7.					
8.					
9.					
10.					
11.					
12.					

The Blue Mosque

The Blue Mosque (Sultan Ahmed Mosque) is located next to the Hagia Sophia in Fatih, İstanbul. This mosque was finished in 1616.

QR code Help File

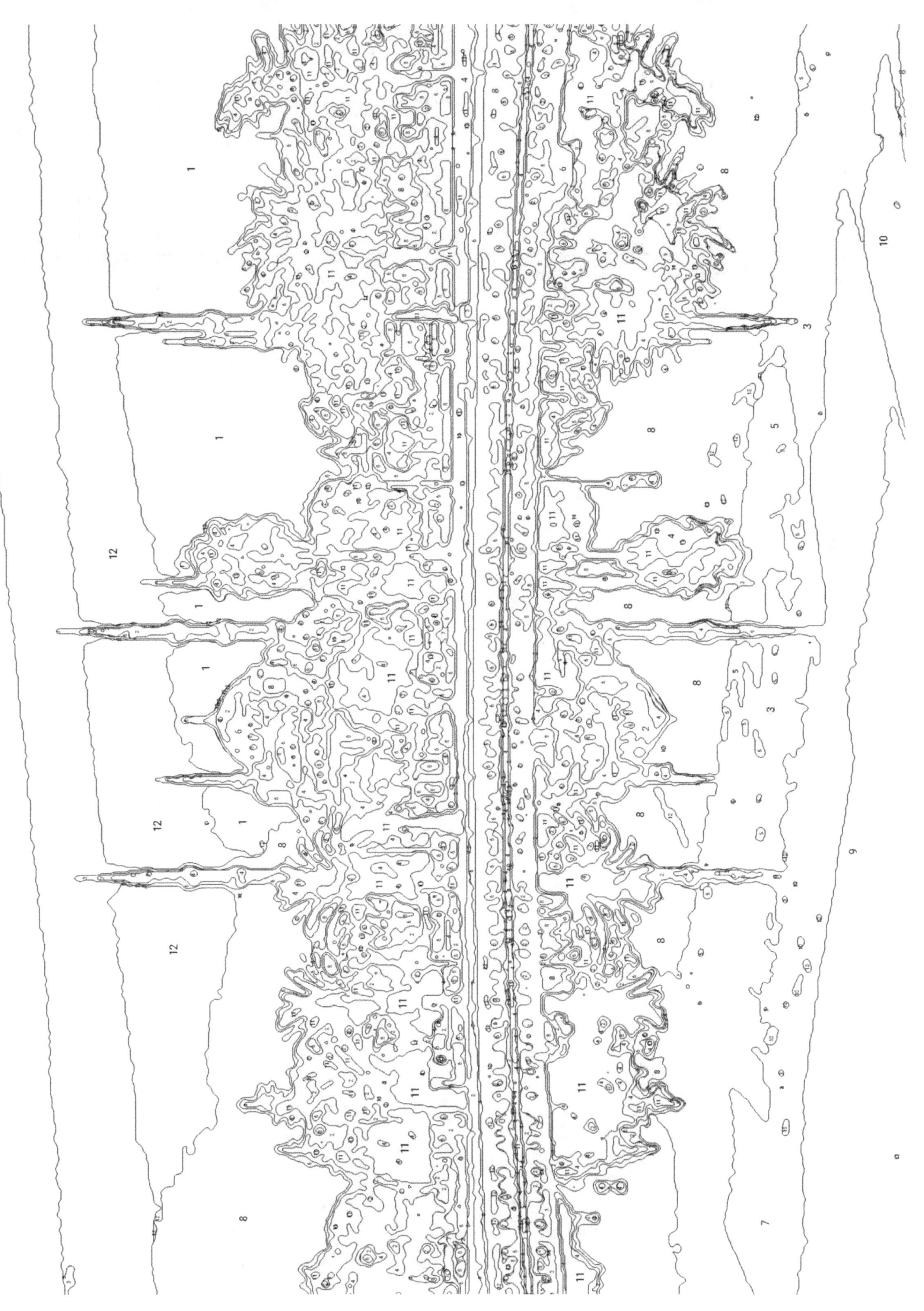

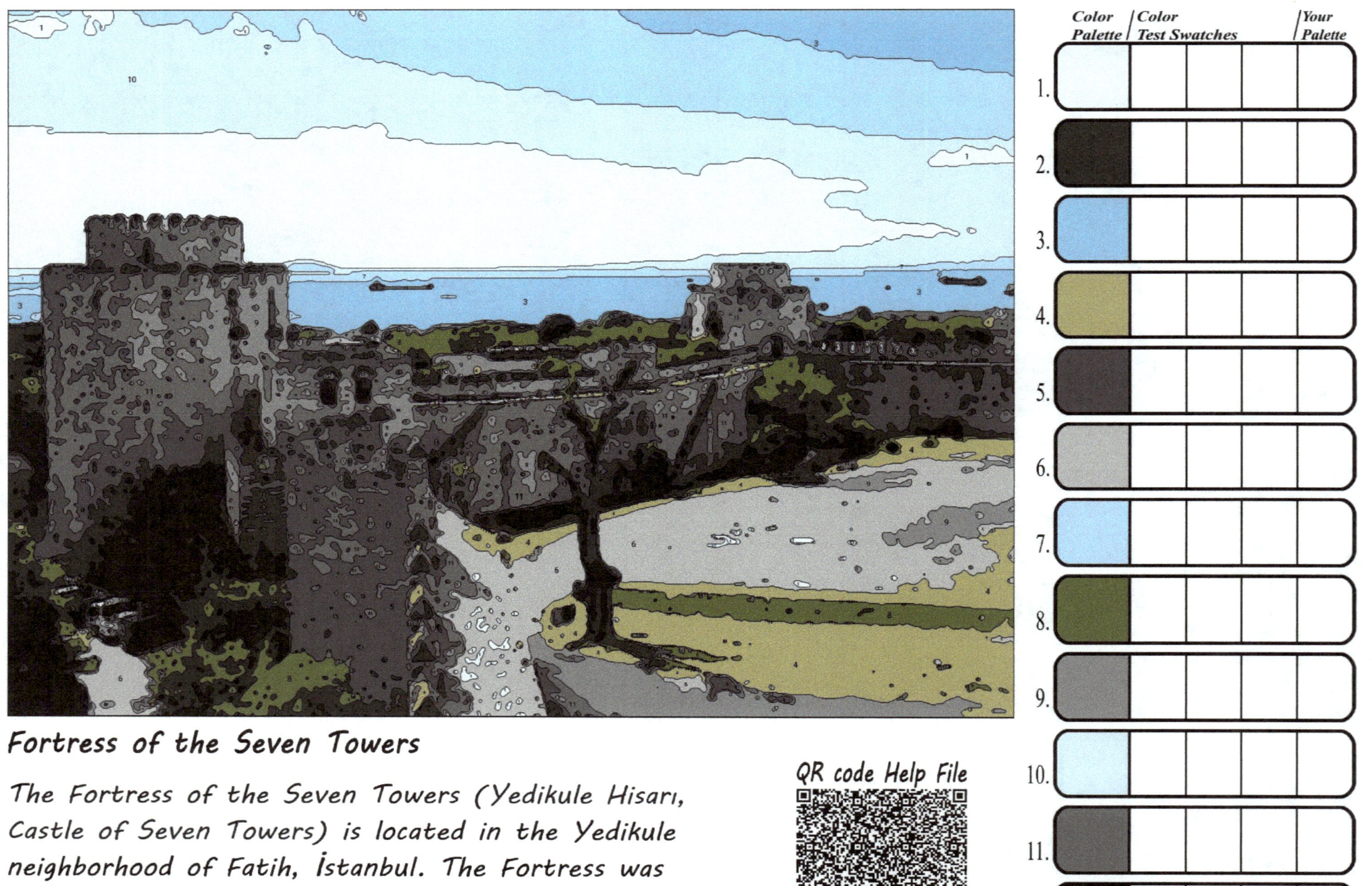

Fortress of the Seven Towers

The Fortress of the Seven Towers (Yedikule Hisarı, Castle of Seven Towers) is located in the Yedikule neighborhood of Fatih, İstanbul. The Fortress was built in 1458, commissioned by Ottoman Sultan Mehmed II.

QR code Help File

	Color Palette	Color Test Swatches			Your Palette
1.					
2.					
3.					
4.					
5.					
6.					
7.					
8.					
9.					
10.					
11.					
12.					

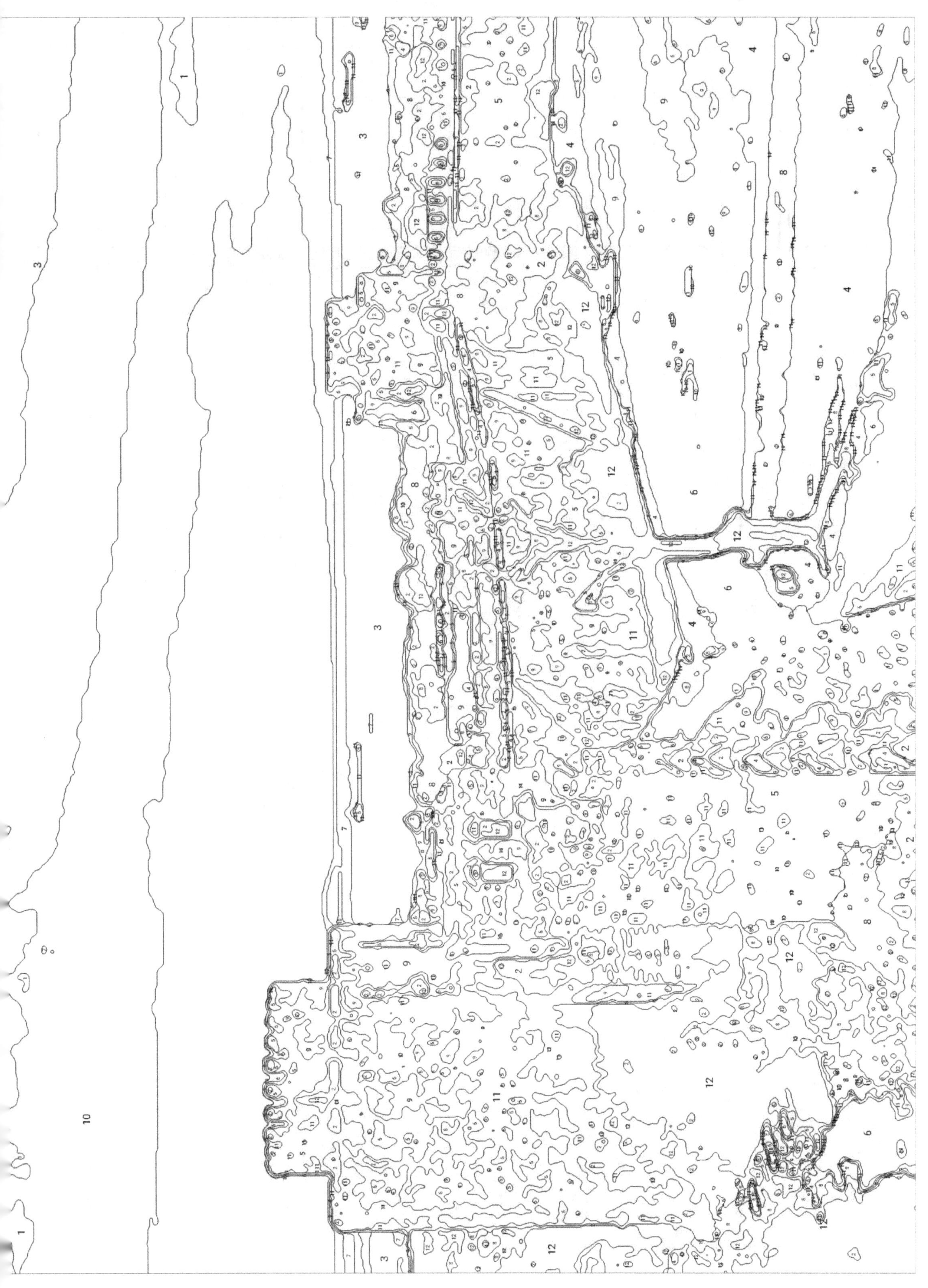

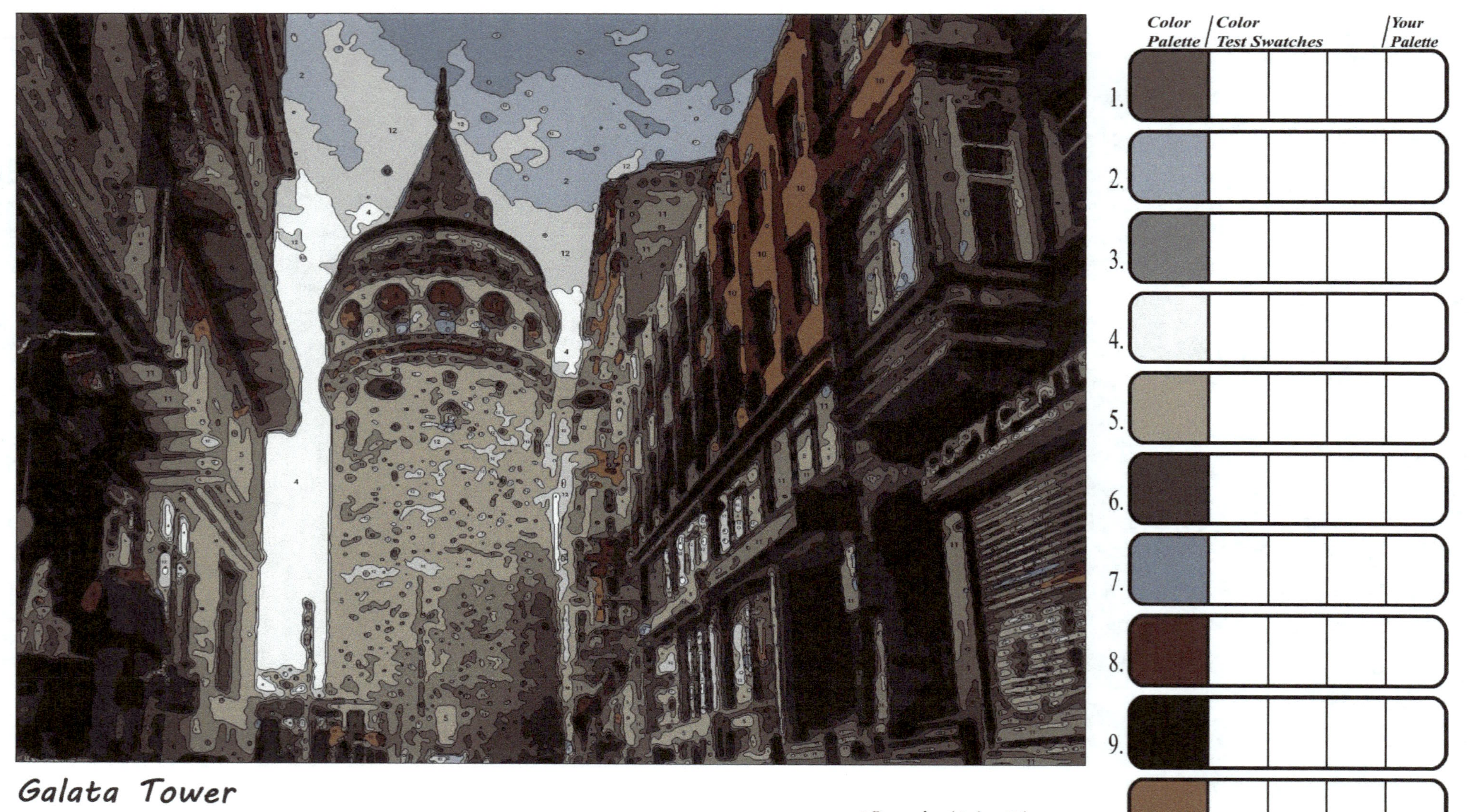

Galata Tower

The Galata Tower is located in the Galata, Karaköy neighborhood in İstanbul. It was built in 1348 and is one of the oldest towers in the world.

QR code Help File

	Color Palette	Color Test Swatches			Your Palette
1.					
2.					
3.					
4.					
5.					
6.					
7.					
8.					
9.					
10.					
11.					
12.					

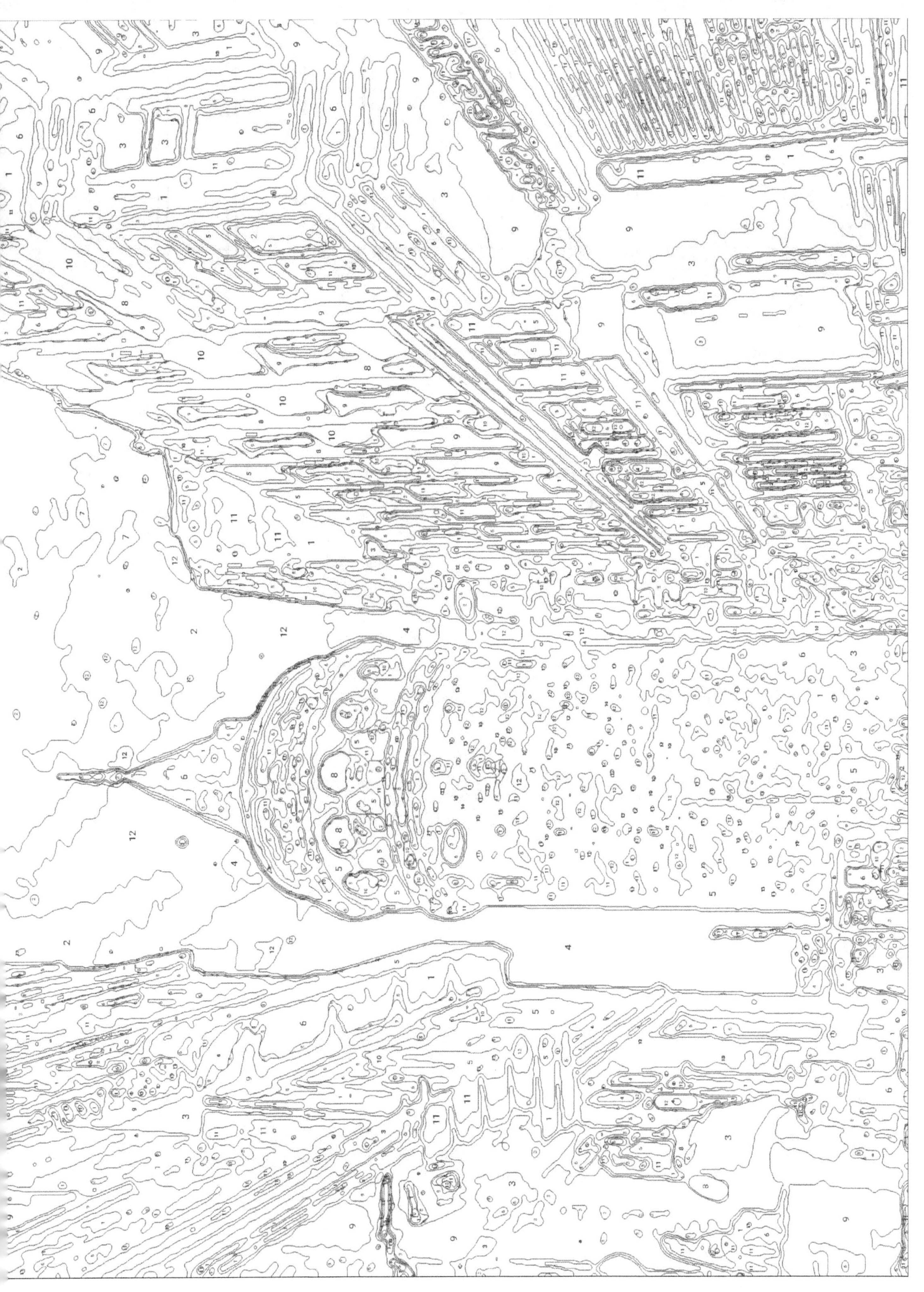

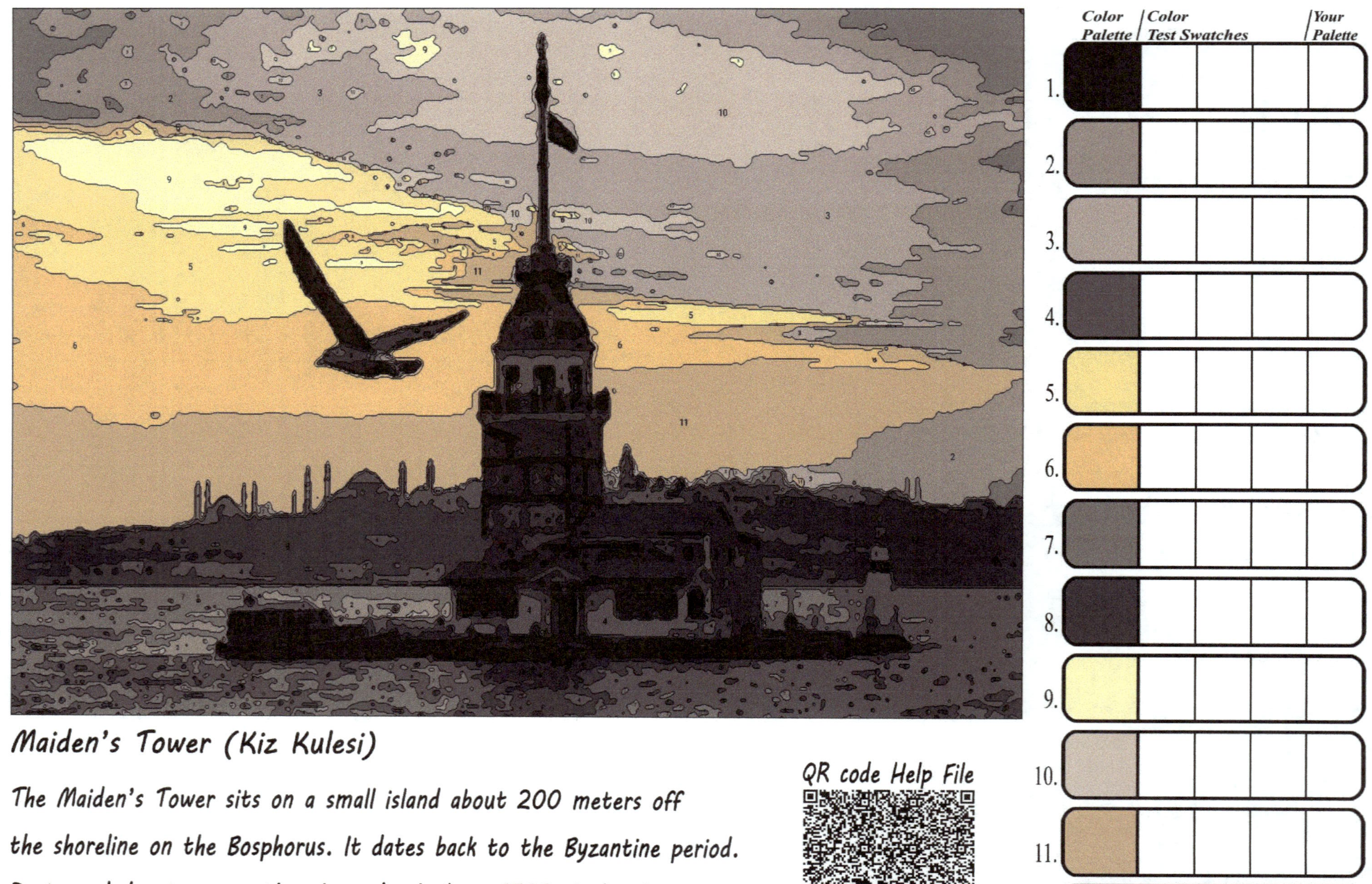

Maiden's Tower (Kiz Kulesi)

The Maiden's Tower sits on a small island about 200 meters off the shoreline on the Bosphorus. It dates back to the Byzantine period. Destroyed due to an earthquake and rebuilt in 1509. It has been used as a Lighthouse and an observation tower.

QR code Help File

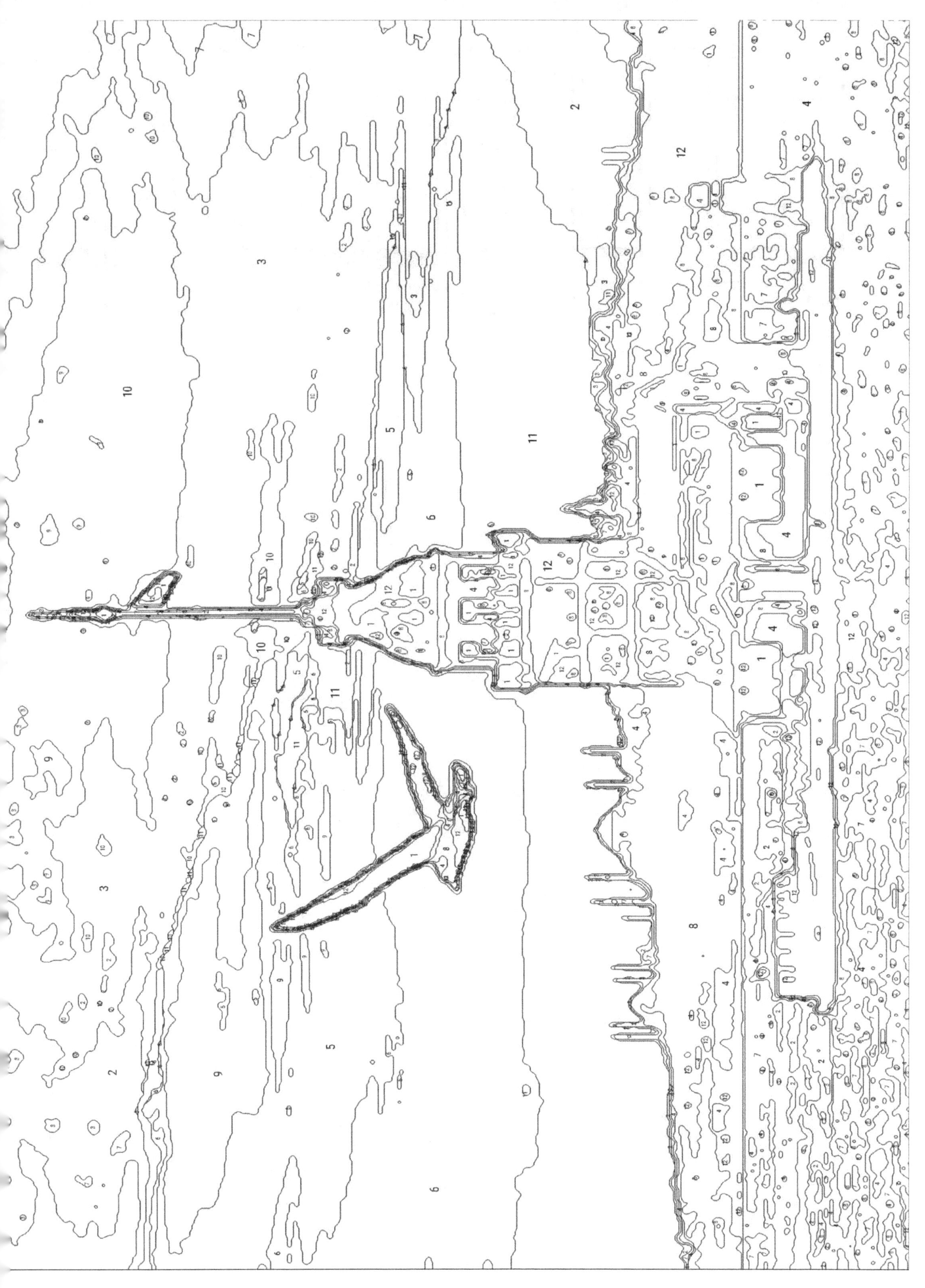

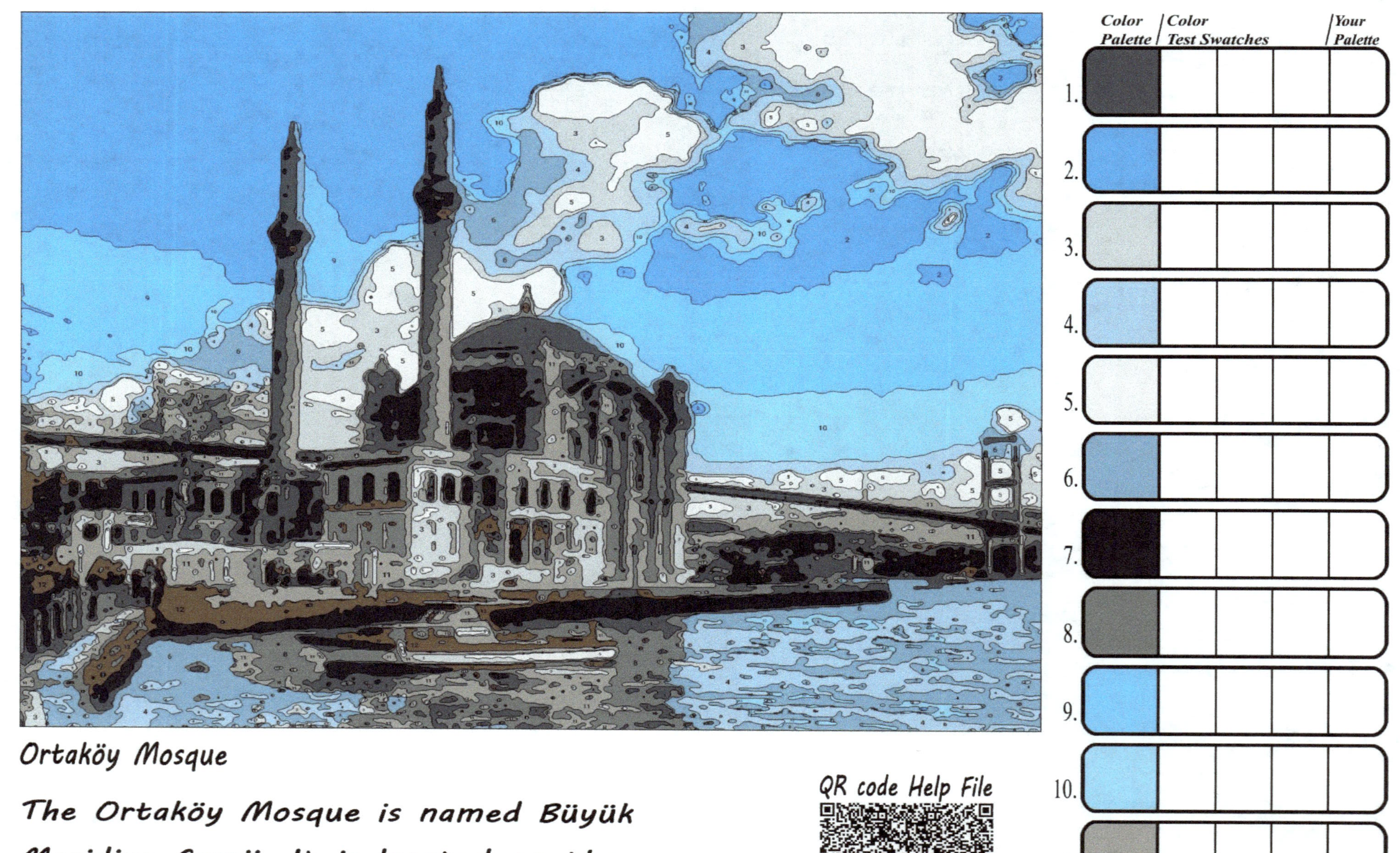

Ortaköy Mosque

The Ortaköy Mosque is named Büyük Mecidiye Camii. It is located on the Ortaköy pier, in the Ortaköy neighborhood of İstanbul. It was built in 1720.

QR code Help File

	Color Palette	Color Test Swatches			Your Palette
1.					
2.					
3.					
4.					
5.					
6.					
7.					
8.					
9.					
10.					
11.					
12.					

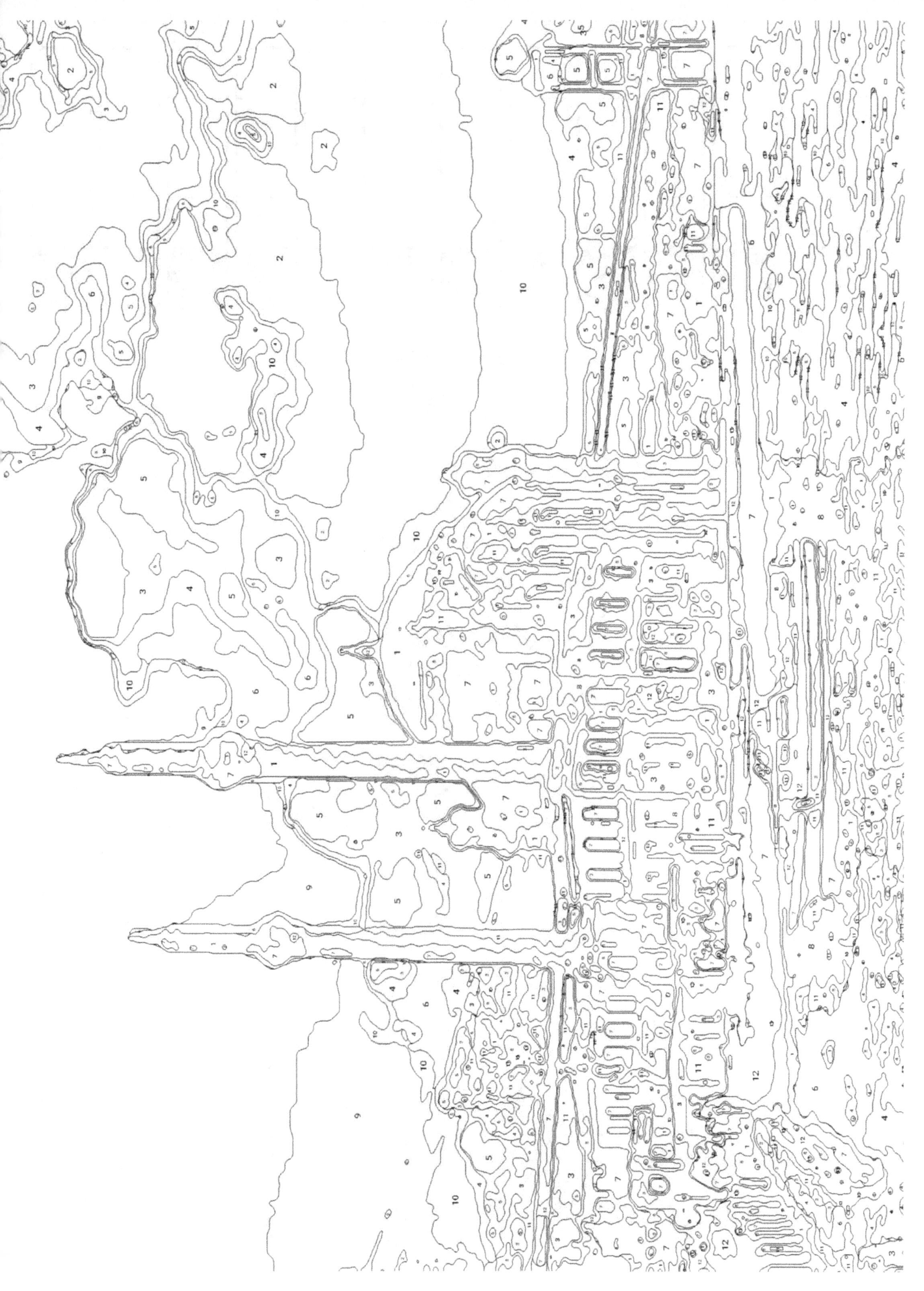

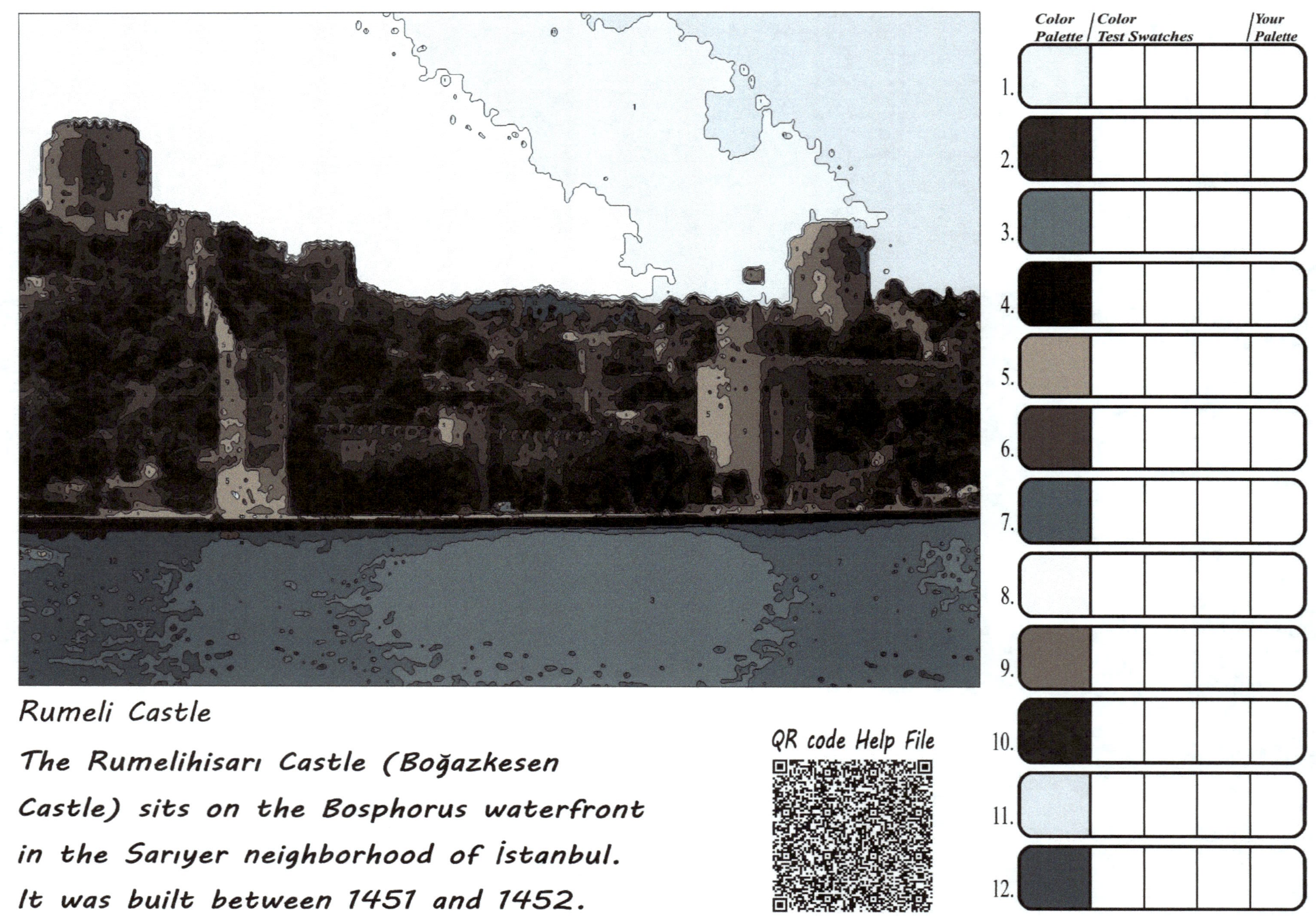

	Color Palette	Color Test Swatches			Your Palette
1.					
2.					
3.					
4.					
5.					
6.					
7.					
8.					
9.					
10.					
11.					
12.					

Rumeli Castle

The Rumelihisarı Castle (Boğazkesen Castle) sits on the Bosphorus waterfront in the Sarıyer neighborhood of İstanbul. It was built between 1451 and 1452.

QR code Help File

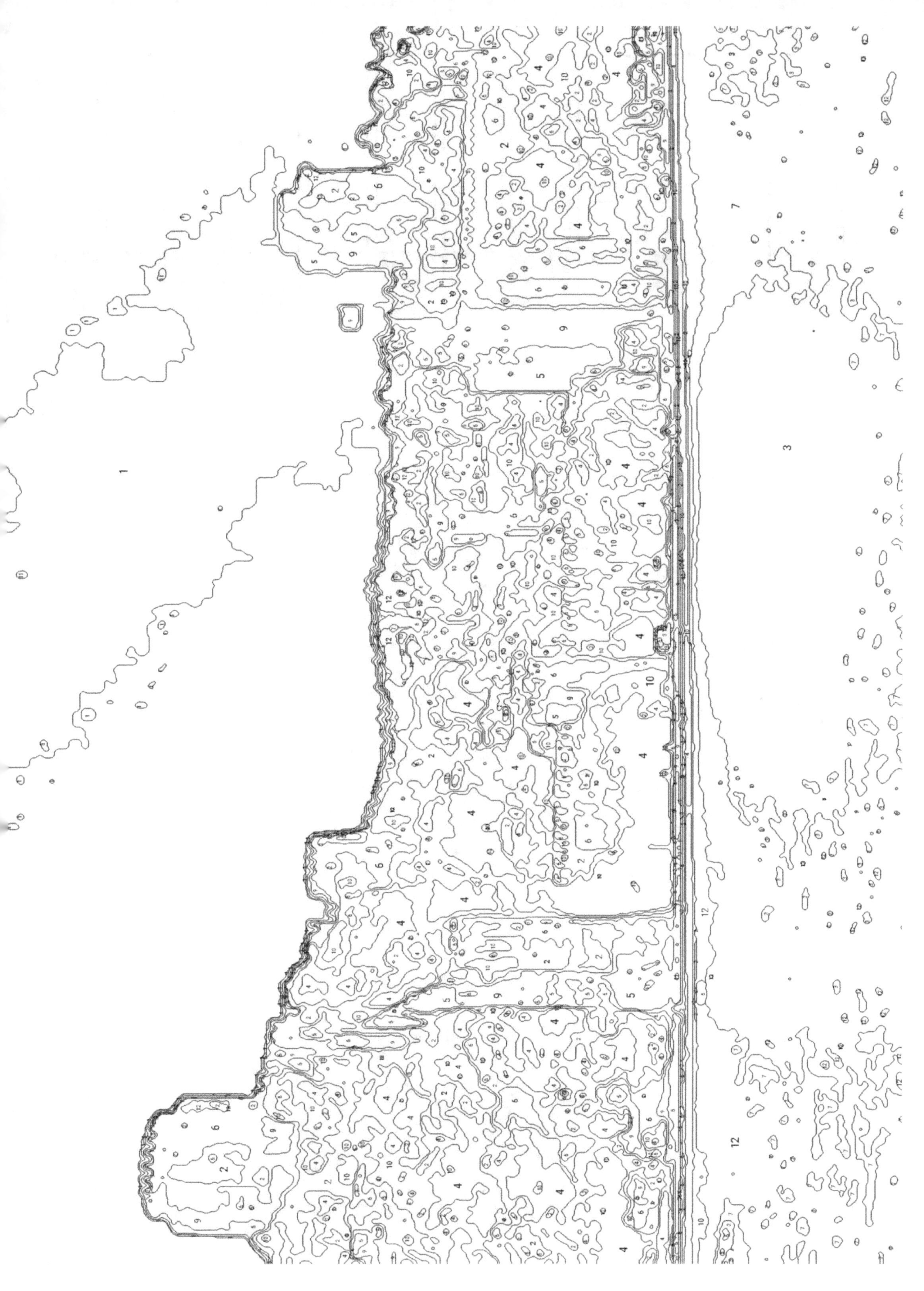

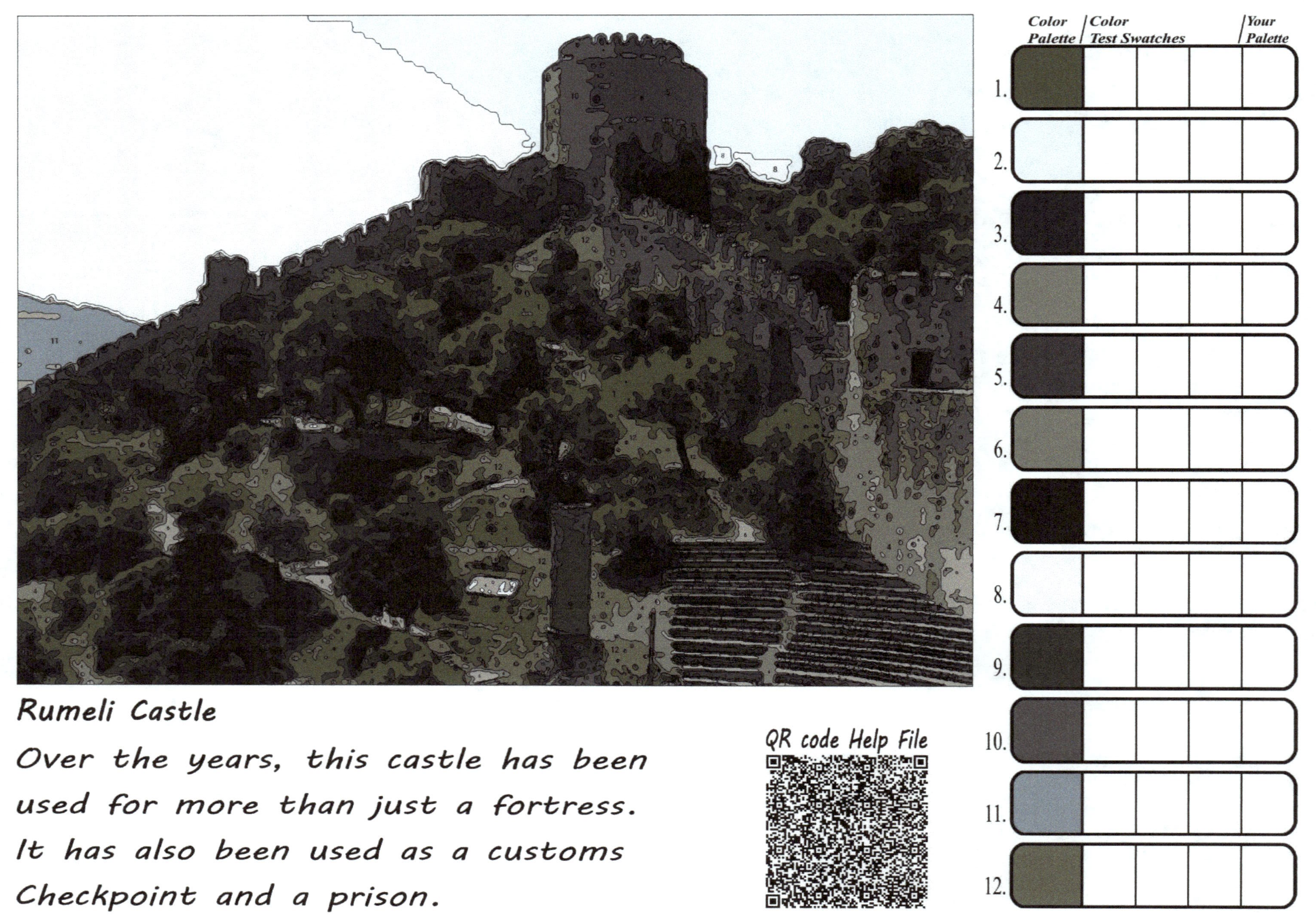

Rumeli Castle

Over the years, this castle has been used for more than just a fortress. It has also been used as a customs Checkpoint and a prison.

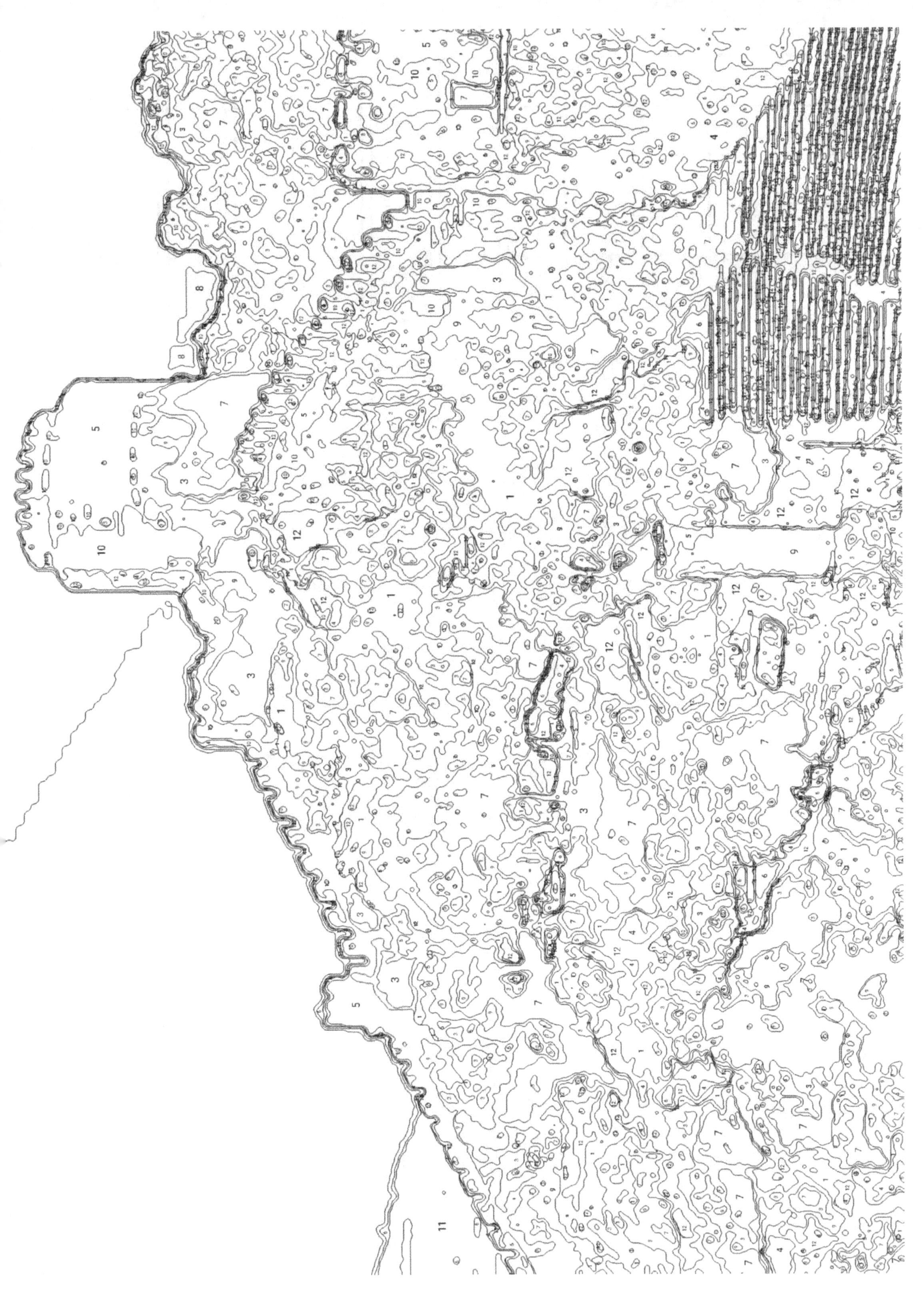

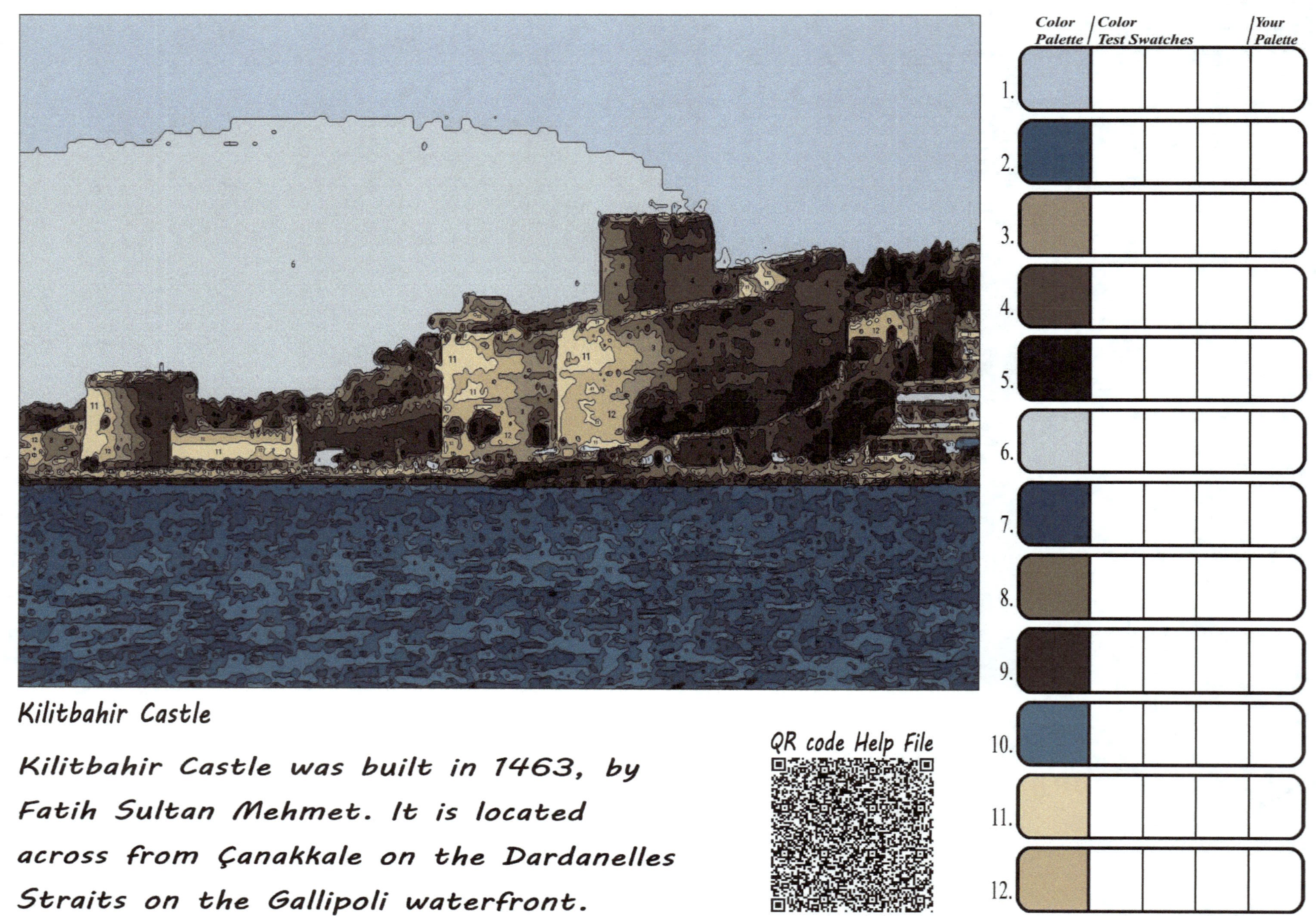

Kilitbahir Castle

Kilitbahir Castle was built in 1463, by Fatih Sultan Mehmet. It is located across from Çanakkale on the Dardanelles Straits on the Gallipoli waterfront.

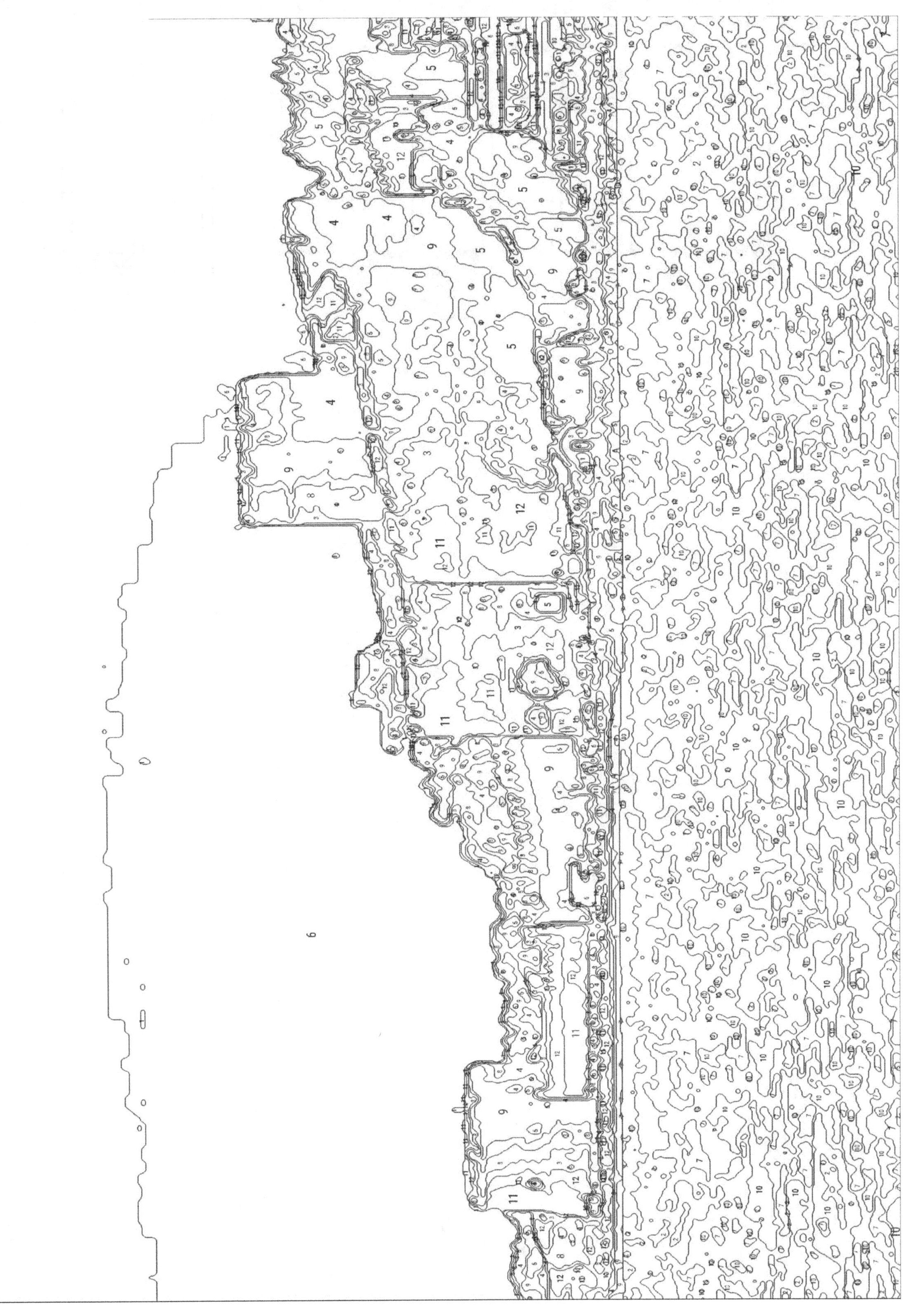

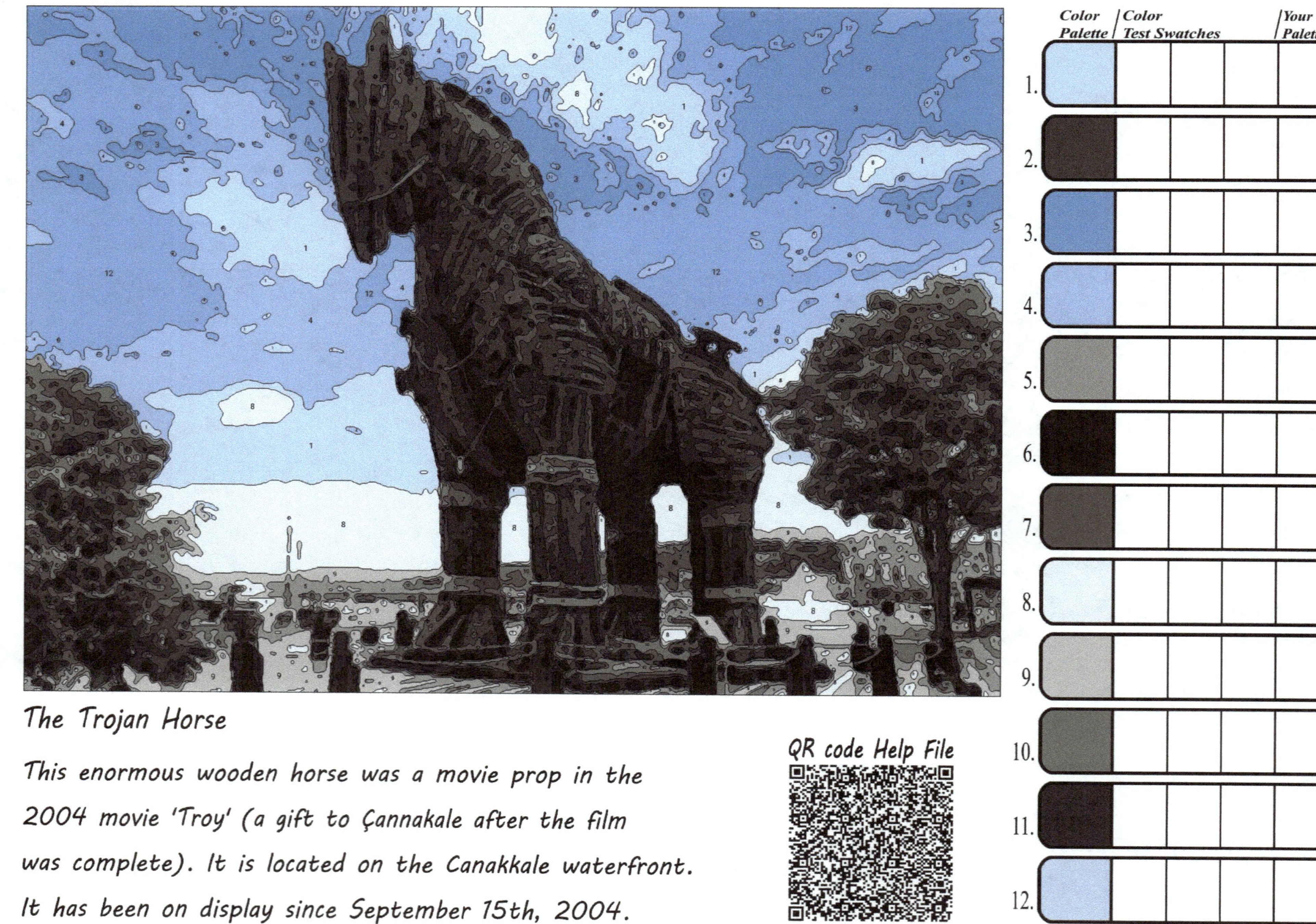

The Trojan Horse

This enormous wooden horse was a movie prop in the 2004 movie 'Troy' (a gift to Çannakale after the film was complete). It is located on the Canakkale waterfront. It has been on display since September 15th, 2004.

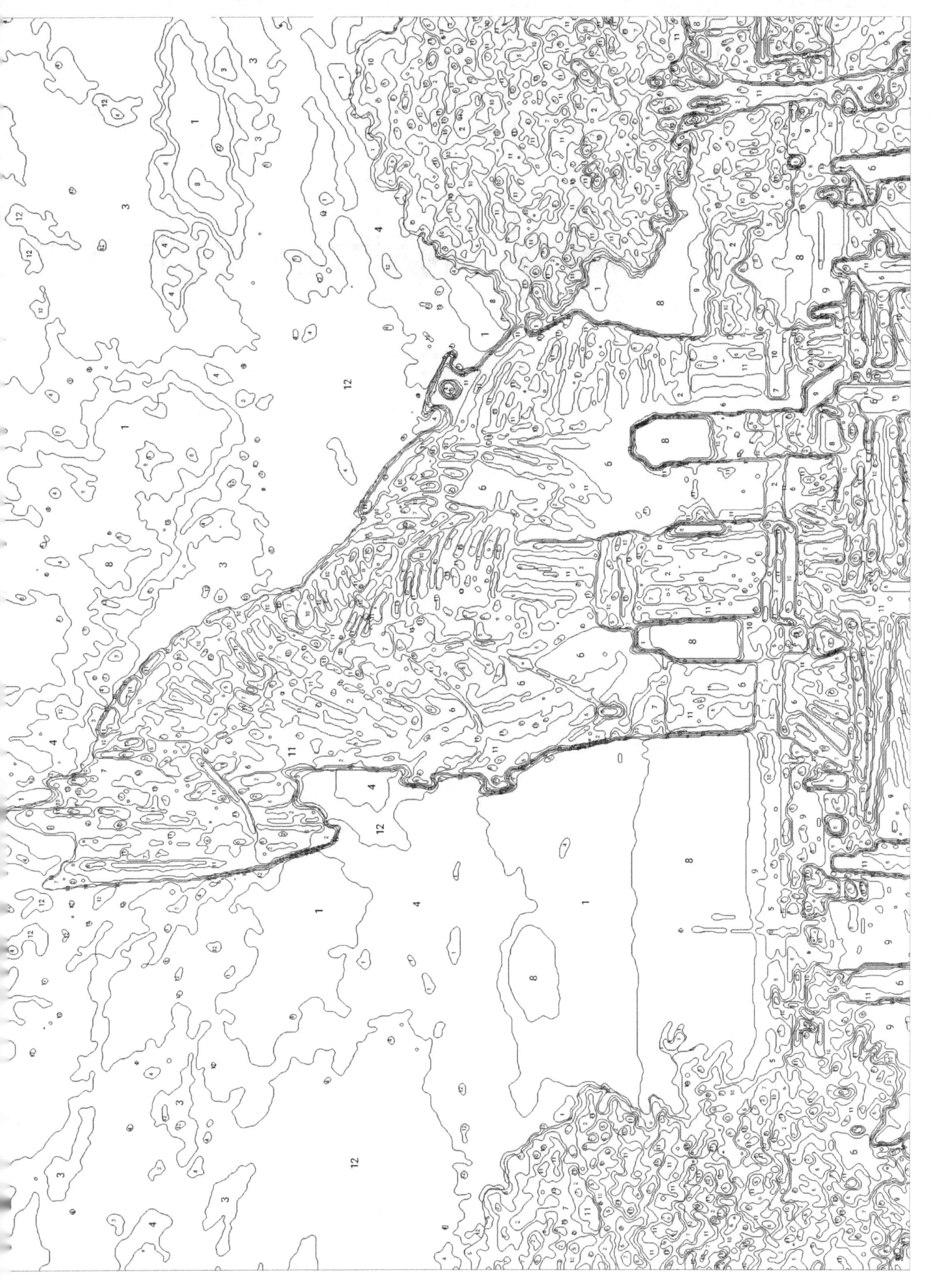

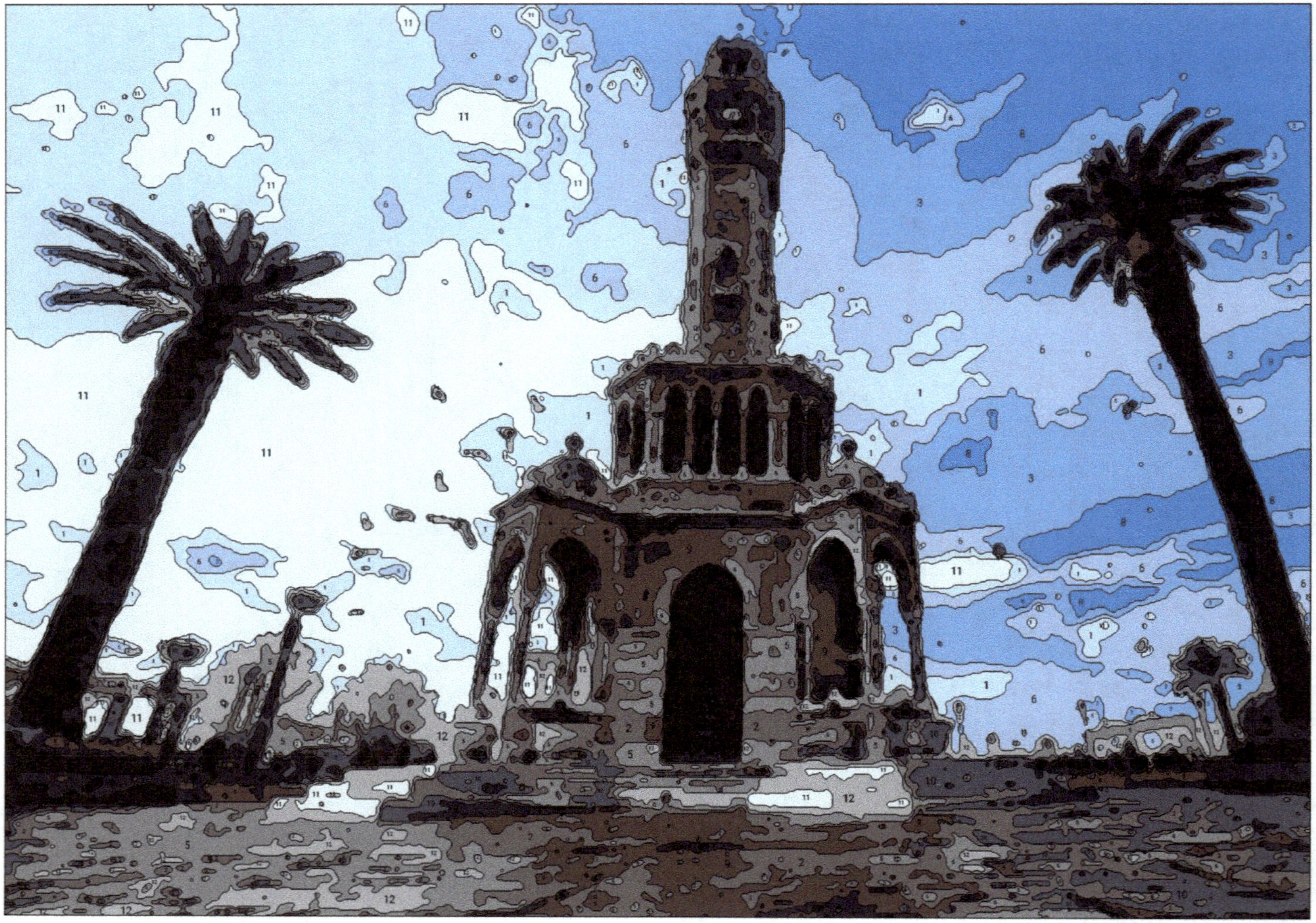

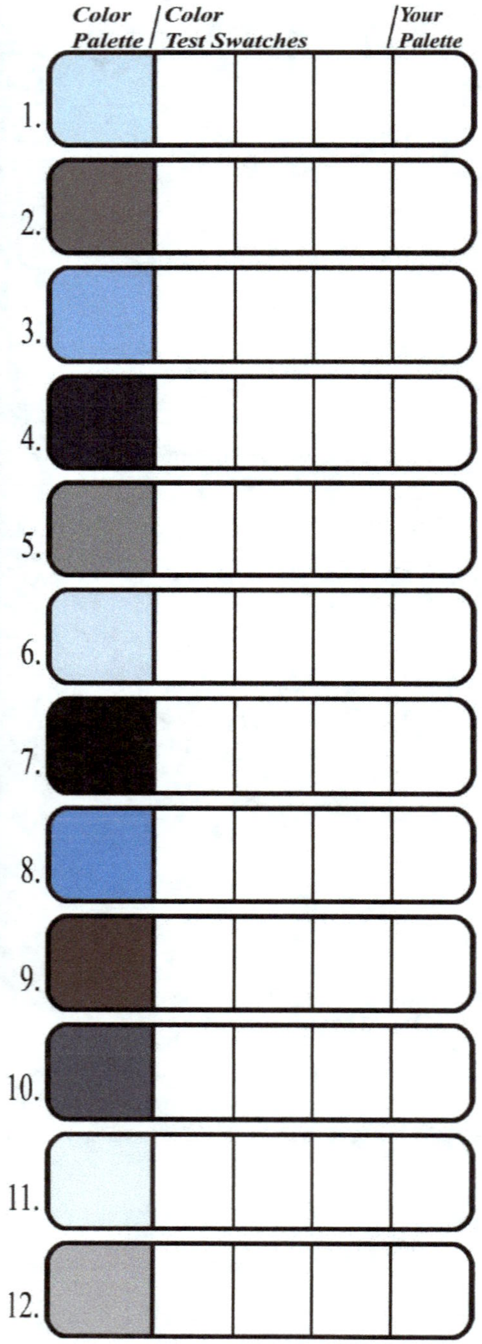

	Color Palette	Color Test Swatches				Your Palette
1.						
2.						
3.						
4.						
5.						
6.						
7.						
8.						
9.						
10.						
11.						
12.						

İzmir Clock Tower

The İzmir Clock Tower is an icon of İzmir, completed in 1901. It is located in the Konak Square in İzmir.

QR code Help File

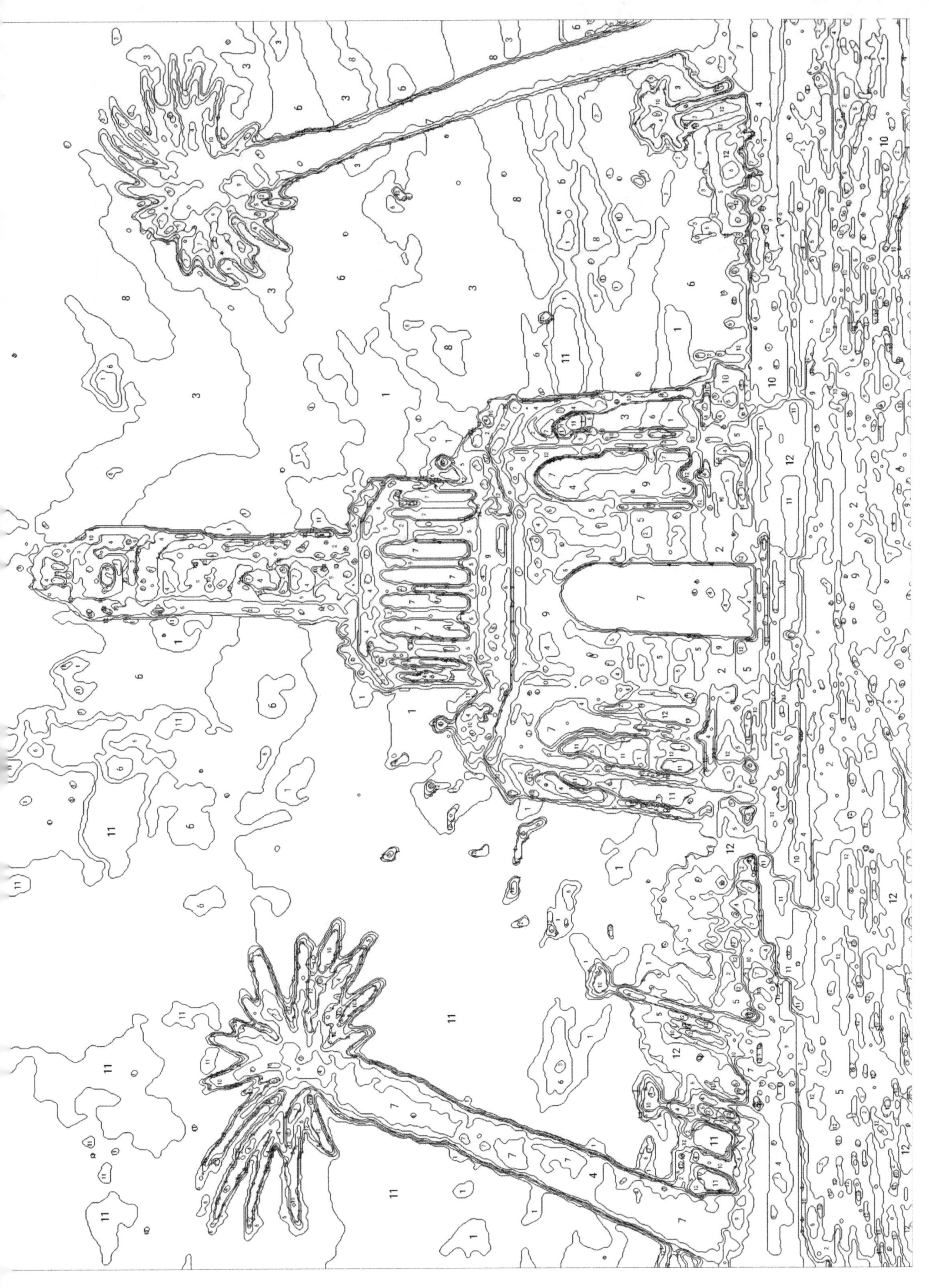

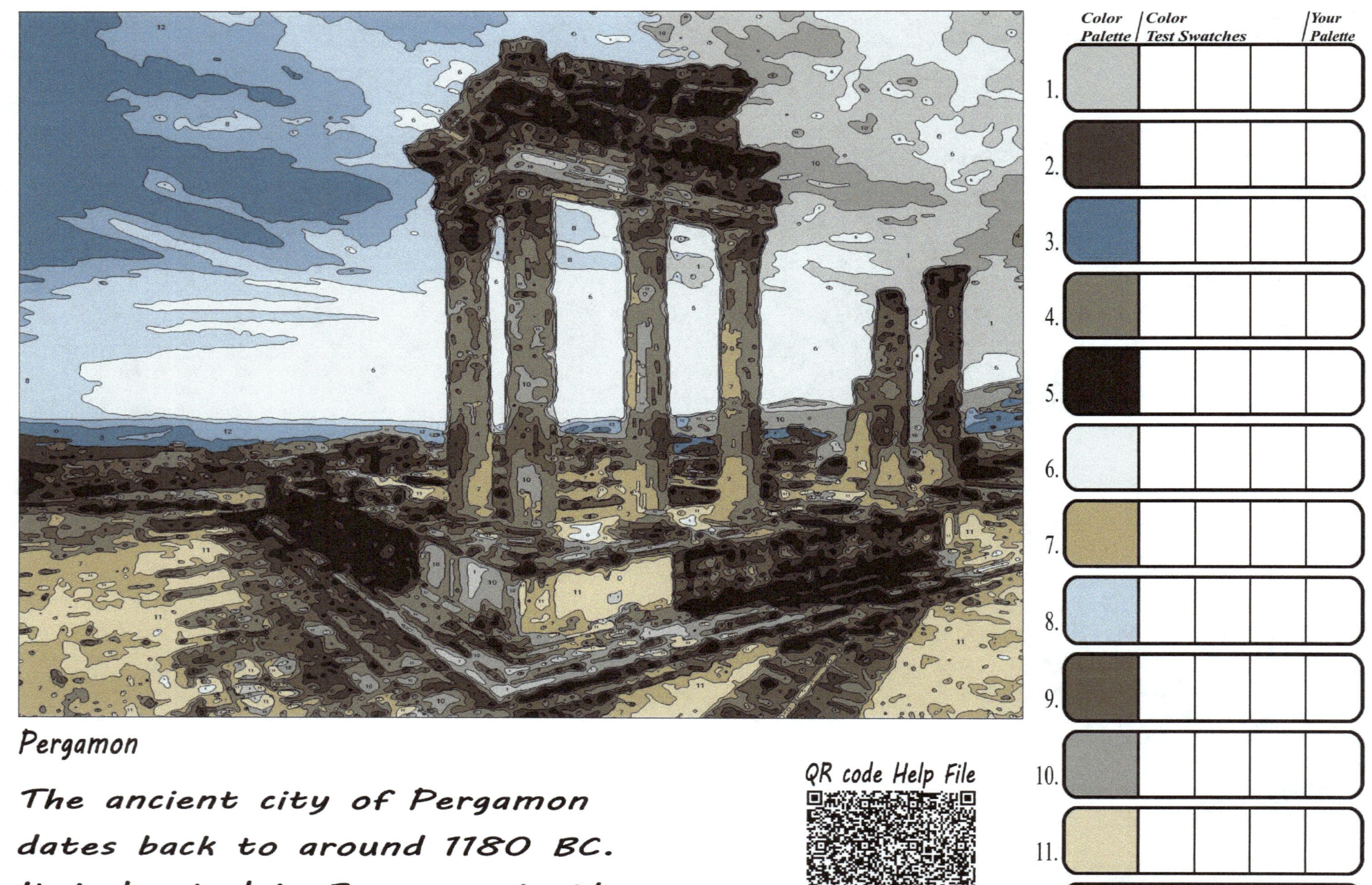

	Color Palette	Color Test Swatches			Your Palette
1.					
2.					
3.					
4.					
5.					
6.					
7.					
8.					
9.					
10.					
11.					
12.					

Pergamon

The ancient city of Pergamon dates back to around 1180 BC. It is located in Bergama, in the İzmir province.

QR code Help File

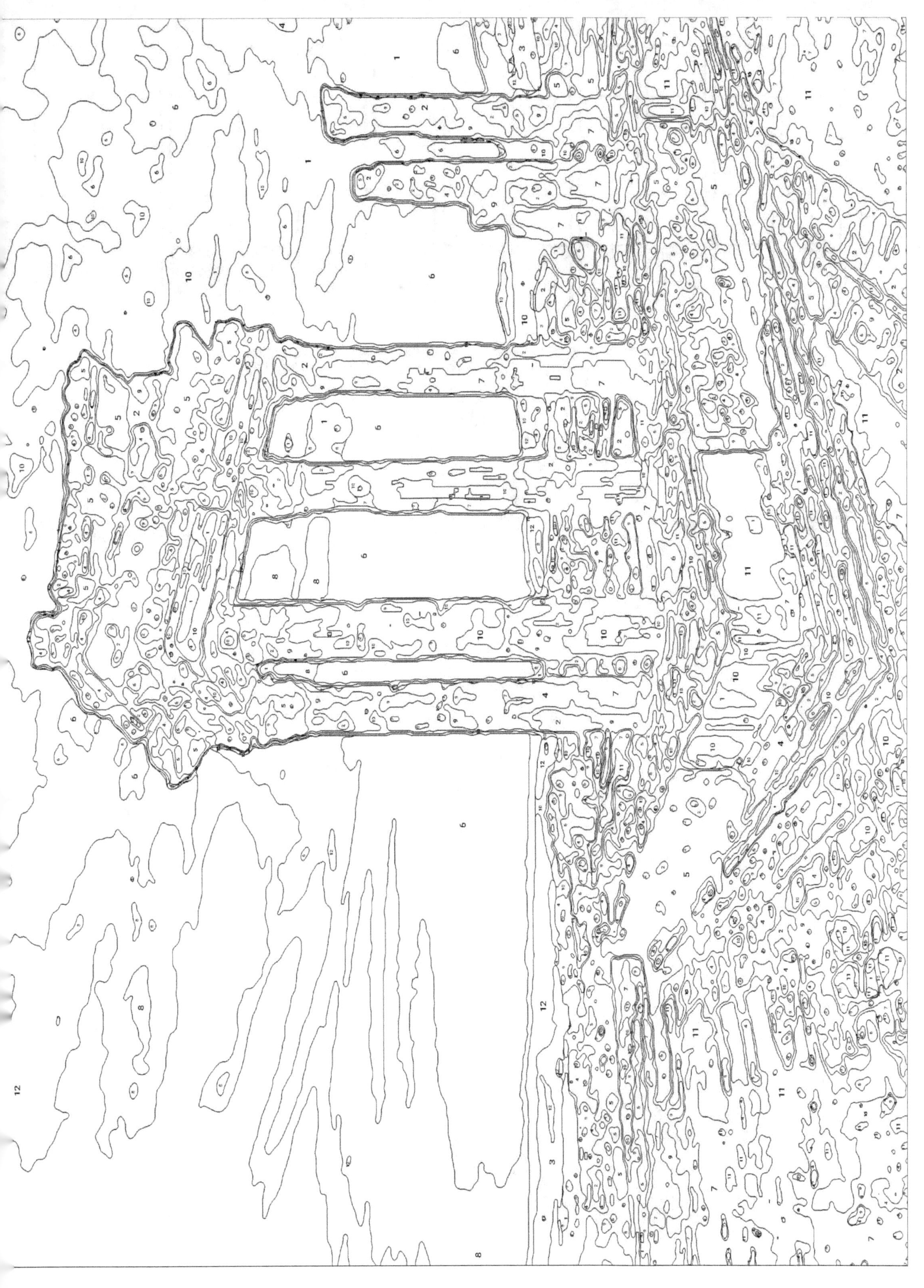

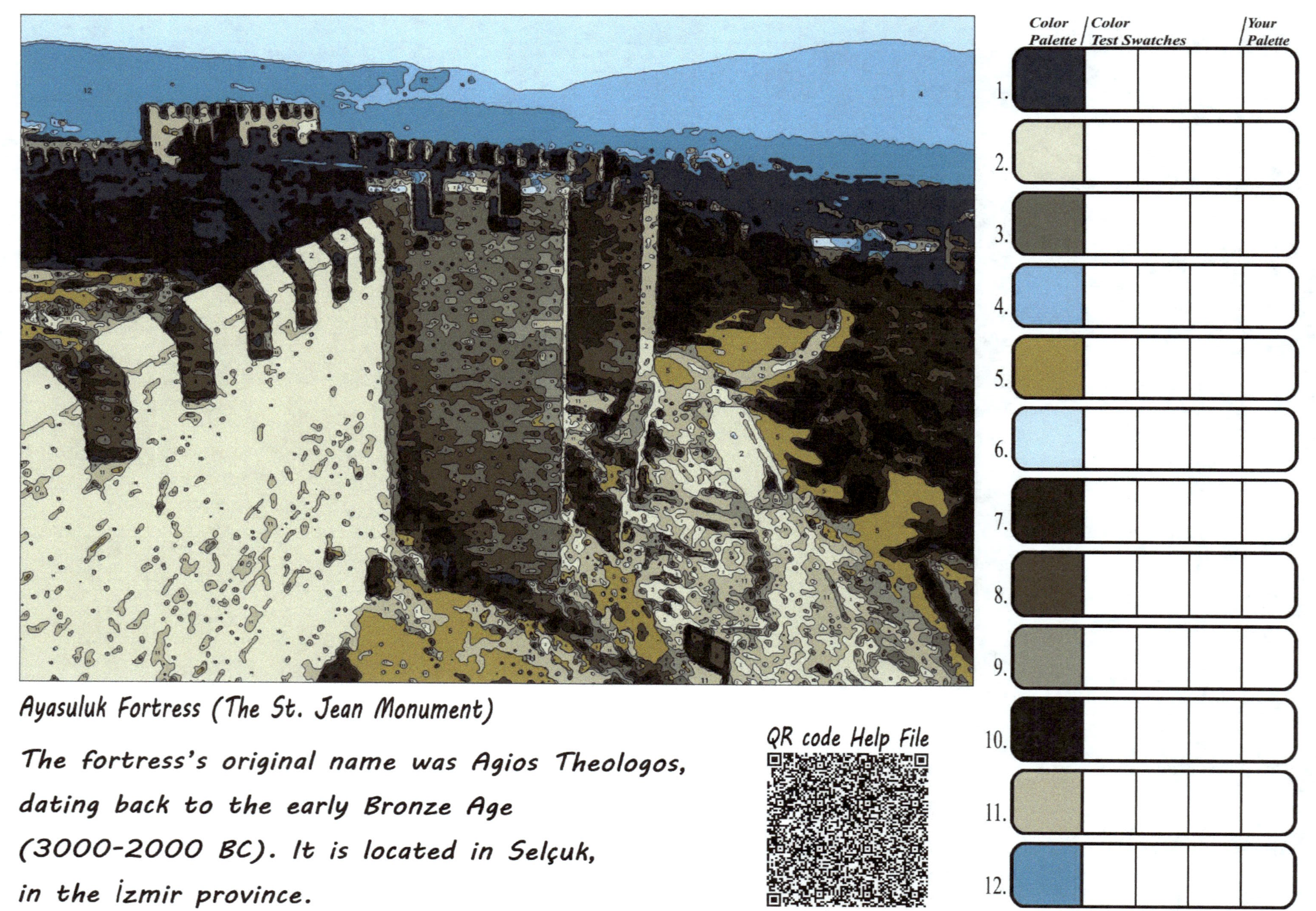

Ayasuluk Fortress (The St. Jean Monument)

The fortress's original name was Agios Theologos, dating back to the early Bronze Age (3000-2000 BC). It is located in Selçuk, in the İzmir province.

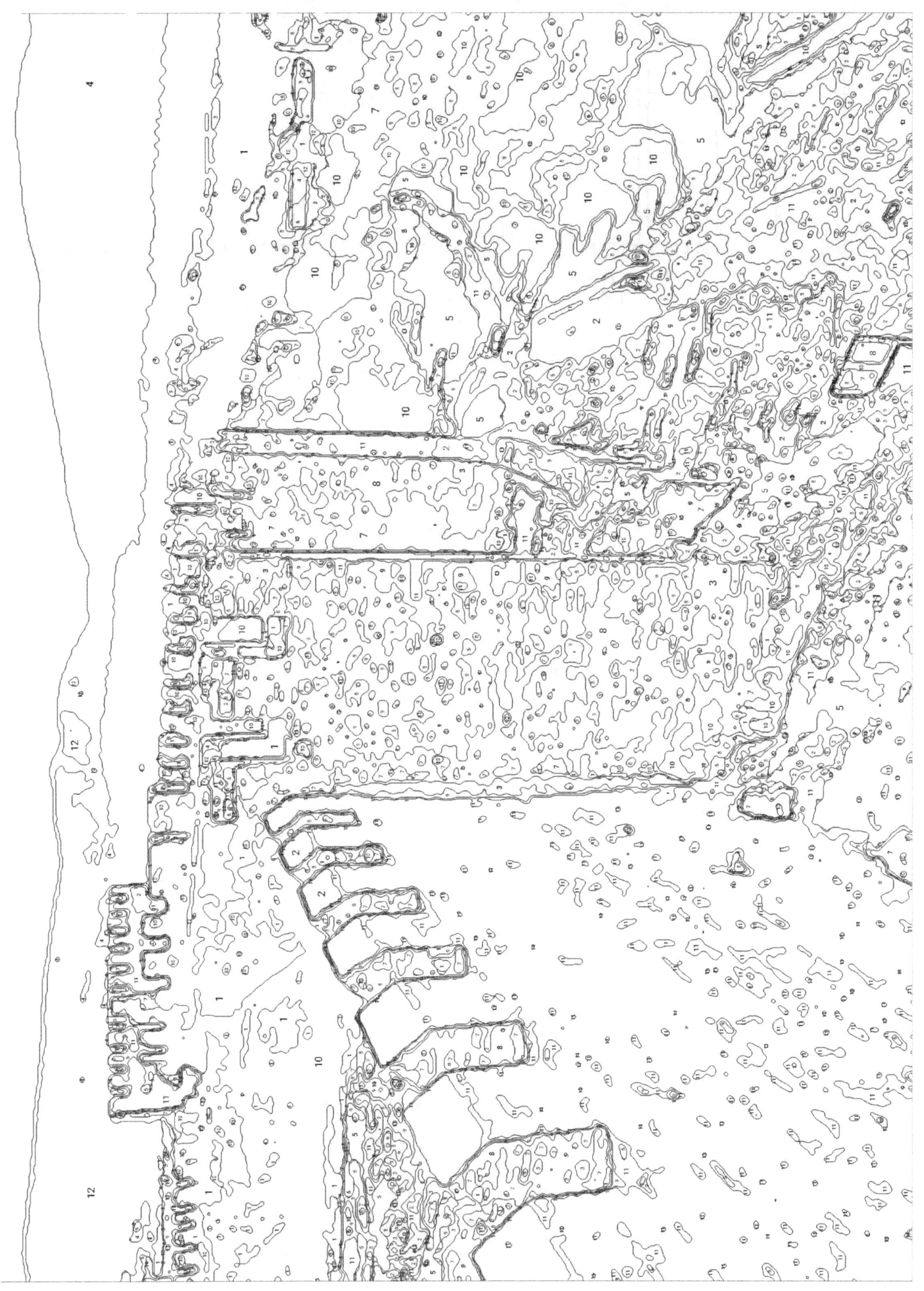

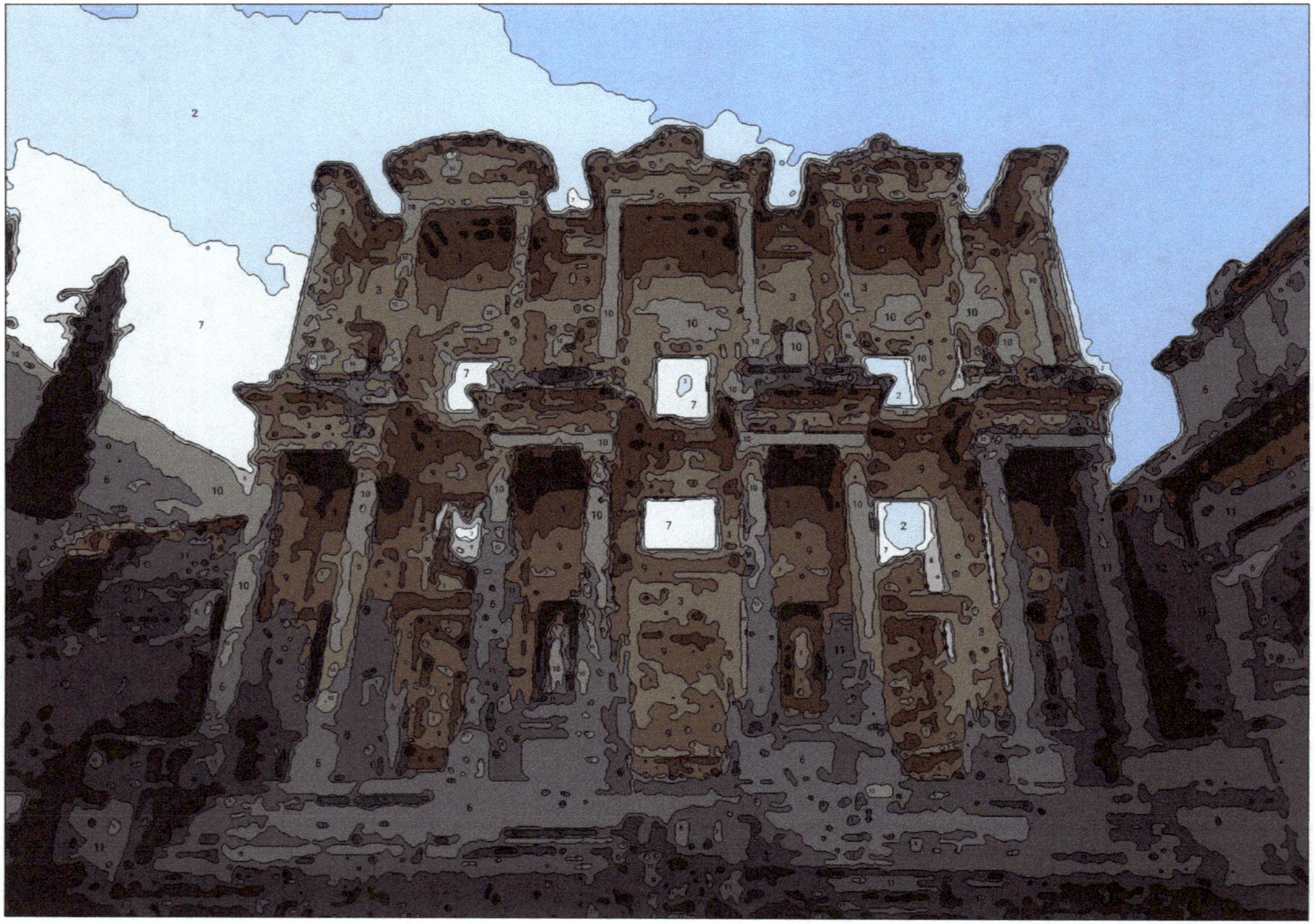

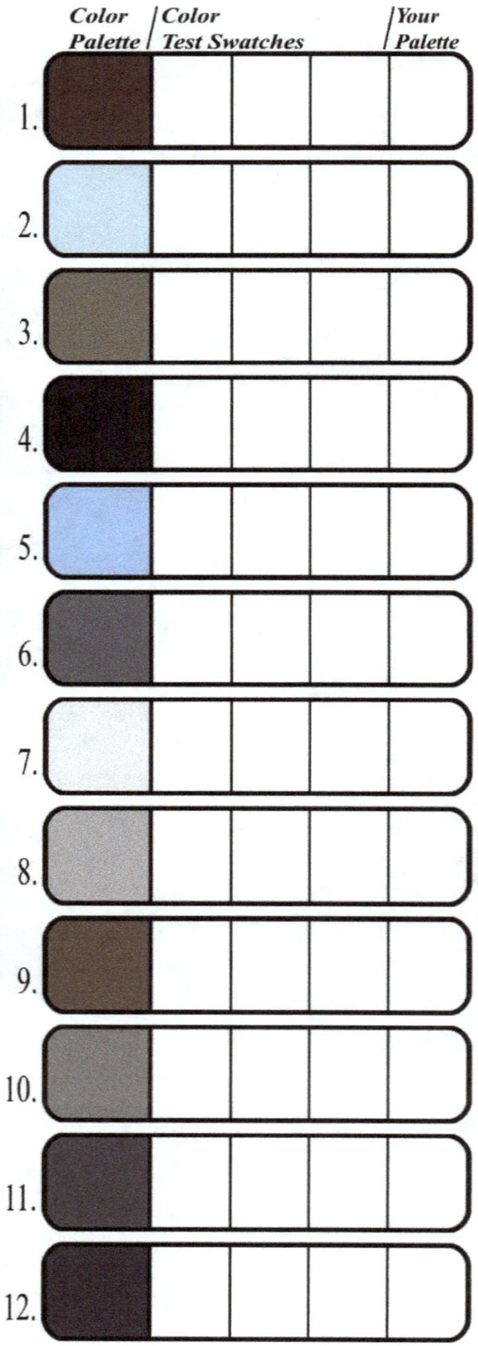

	Color Palette	Color Test Swatches				Your Palette
1.						
2.						
3.						
4.						
5.						
6.						
7.						
8.						
9.						
10.						
11.						
12.						

Library of Celsus

The Library of Celsus was the 3rd largest library in Ancient times. Commissioned in 110 CE. It is located at Ephesus, Selçuk İzmir.

QR code Help File

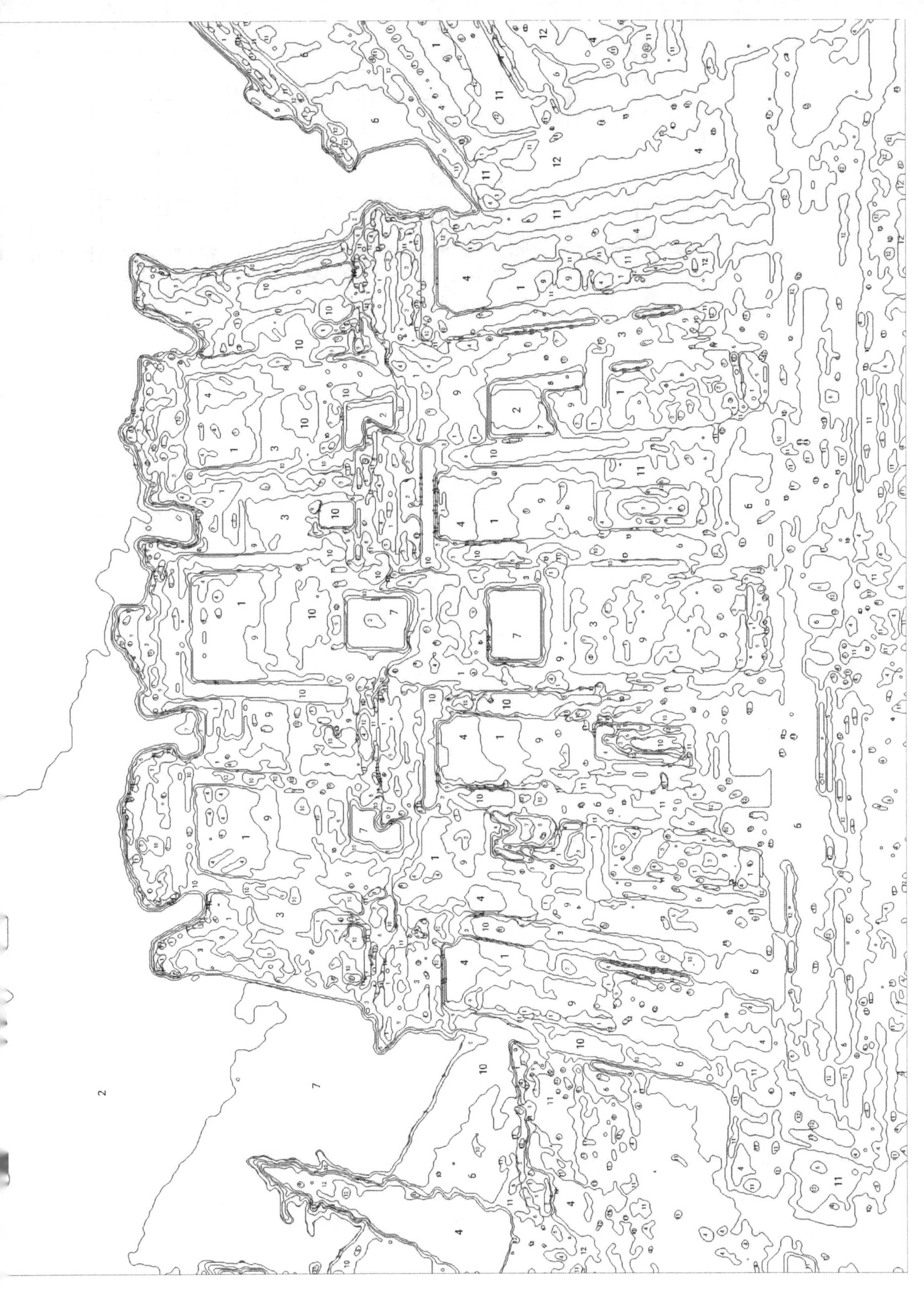

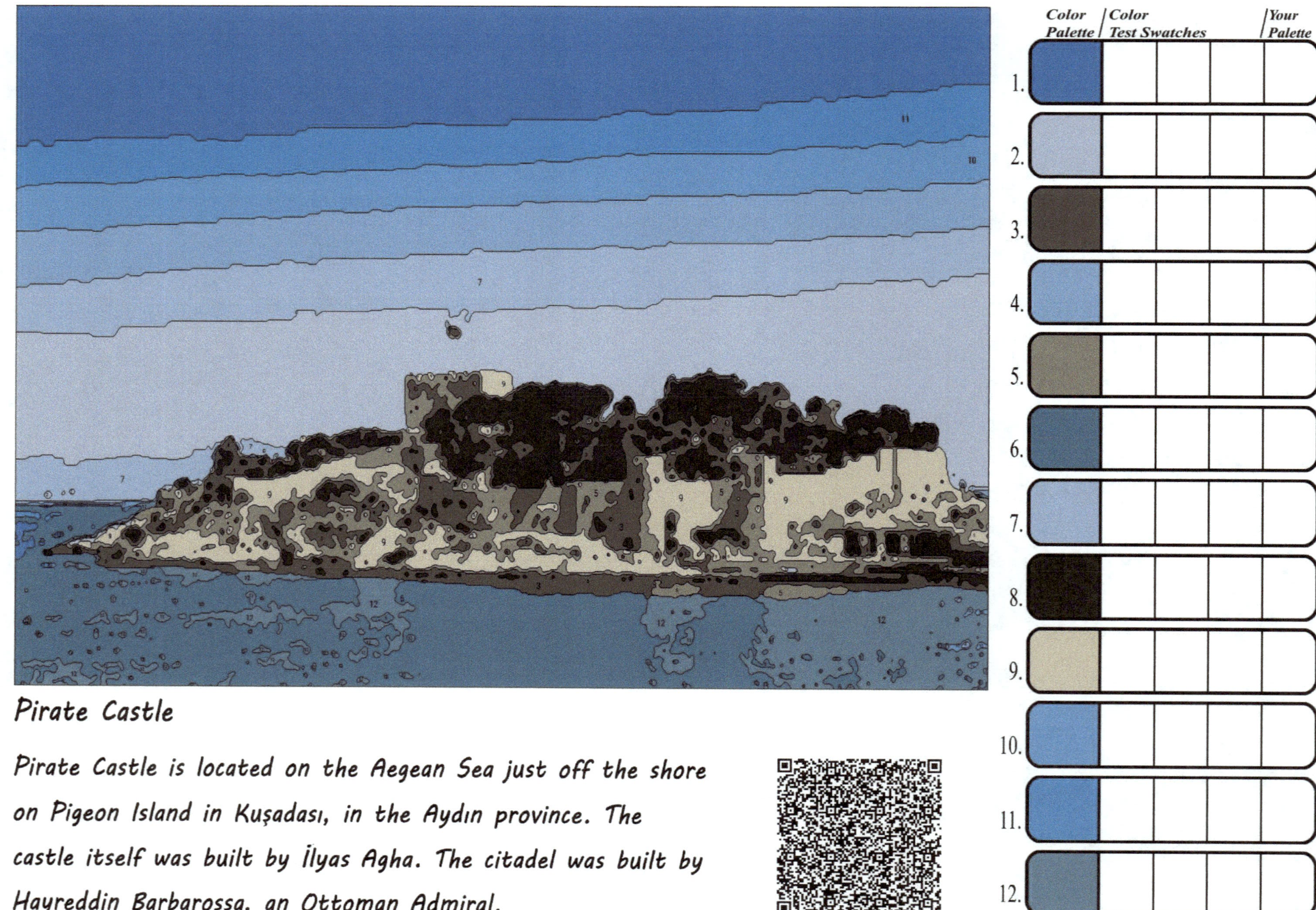

Color Palette	Color Test Swatches			Your Palette
1.				
2.				
3.				
4.				
5.				
6.				
7.				
8.				
9.				
10.				
11.				
12.				

Pirate Castle

Pirate Castle is located on the Aegean Sea just off the shore on Pigeon Island in Kuşadası, in the Aydın province. The castle itself was built by İlyas Agha. The citadel was built by Hayreddin Barbarossa, an Ottoman Admiral.

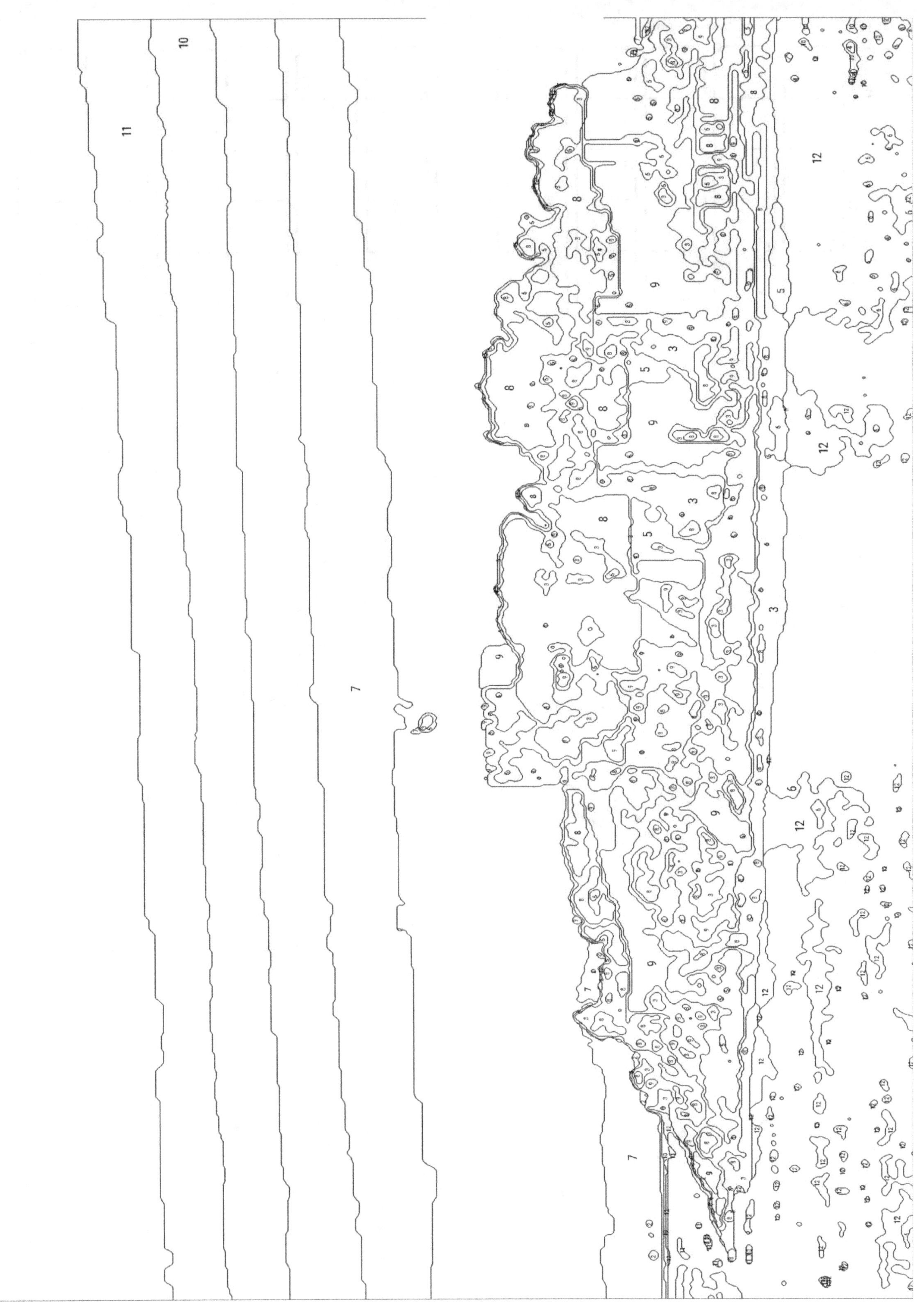

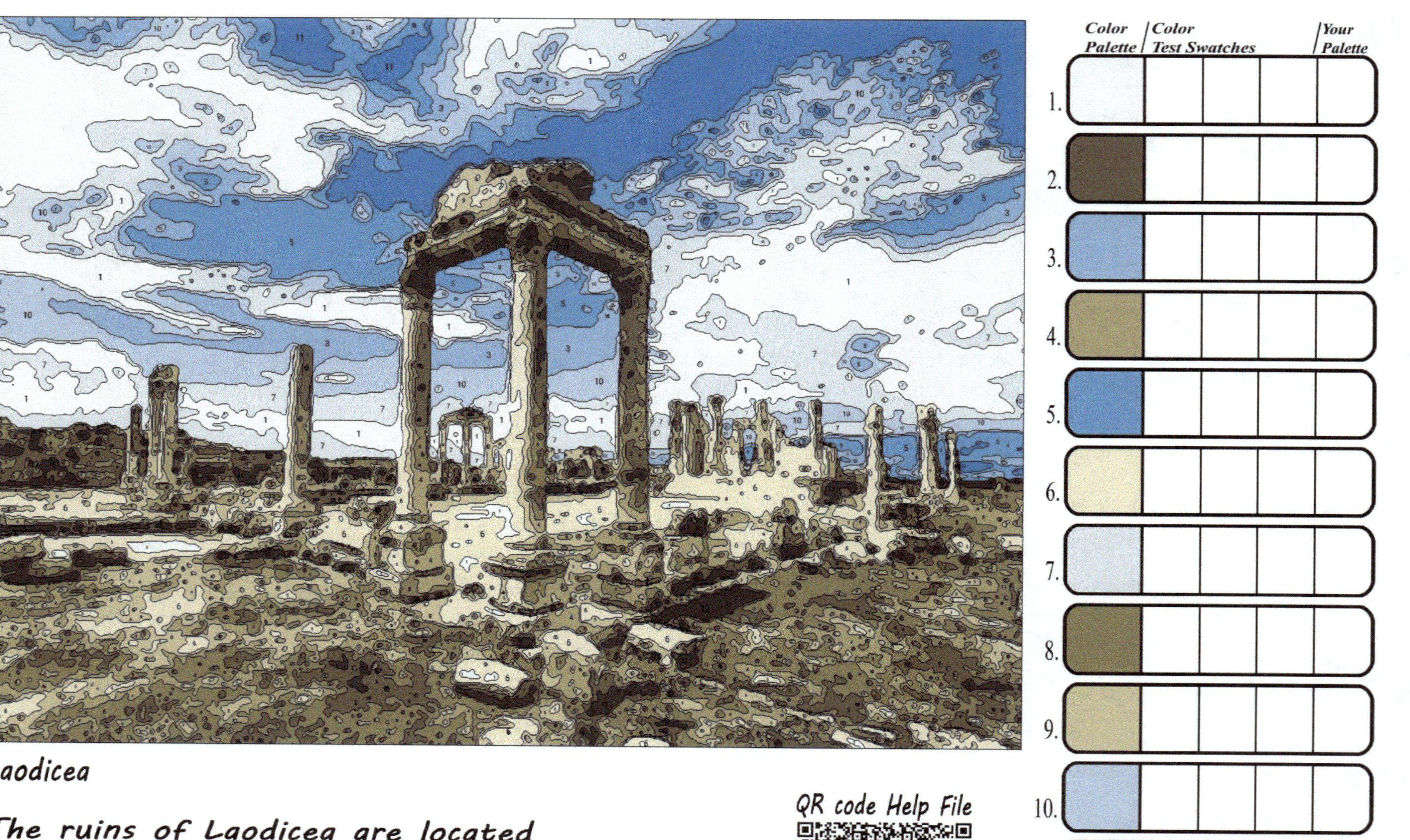

Laodicea

The ruins of Laodicea are located near the village of Goncalı and Eskihisar in the Denizli Province. This ancient city dates back to 5500 BC.

QR code Help File

Color Palette	Color Test Swatches			Your Palette
1.				
2.				
3.				
4.				
5.				
6.				
7.				
8.				
9.				
10.				
11.				
12.				

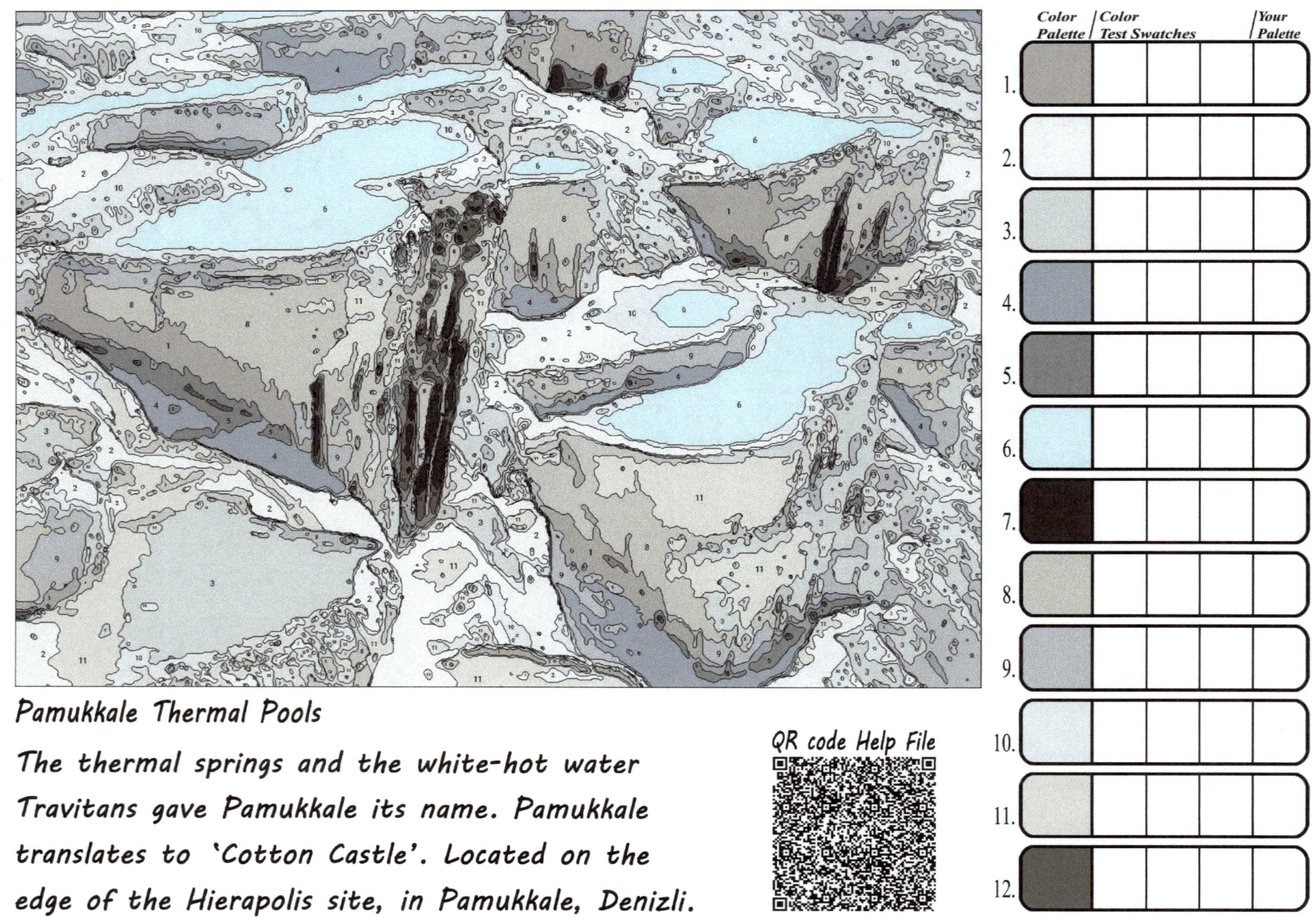

Pamukkale Thermal Pools

The thermal springs and the white-hot water Travitans gave Pamukkale its name. Pamukkale translates to 'Cotton Castle'. Located on the edge of the Hierapolis site, in Pamukkale, Denizli.

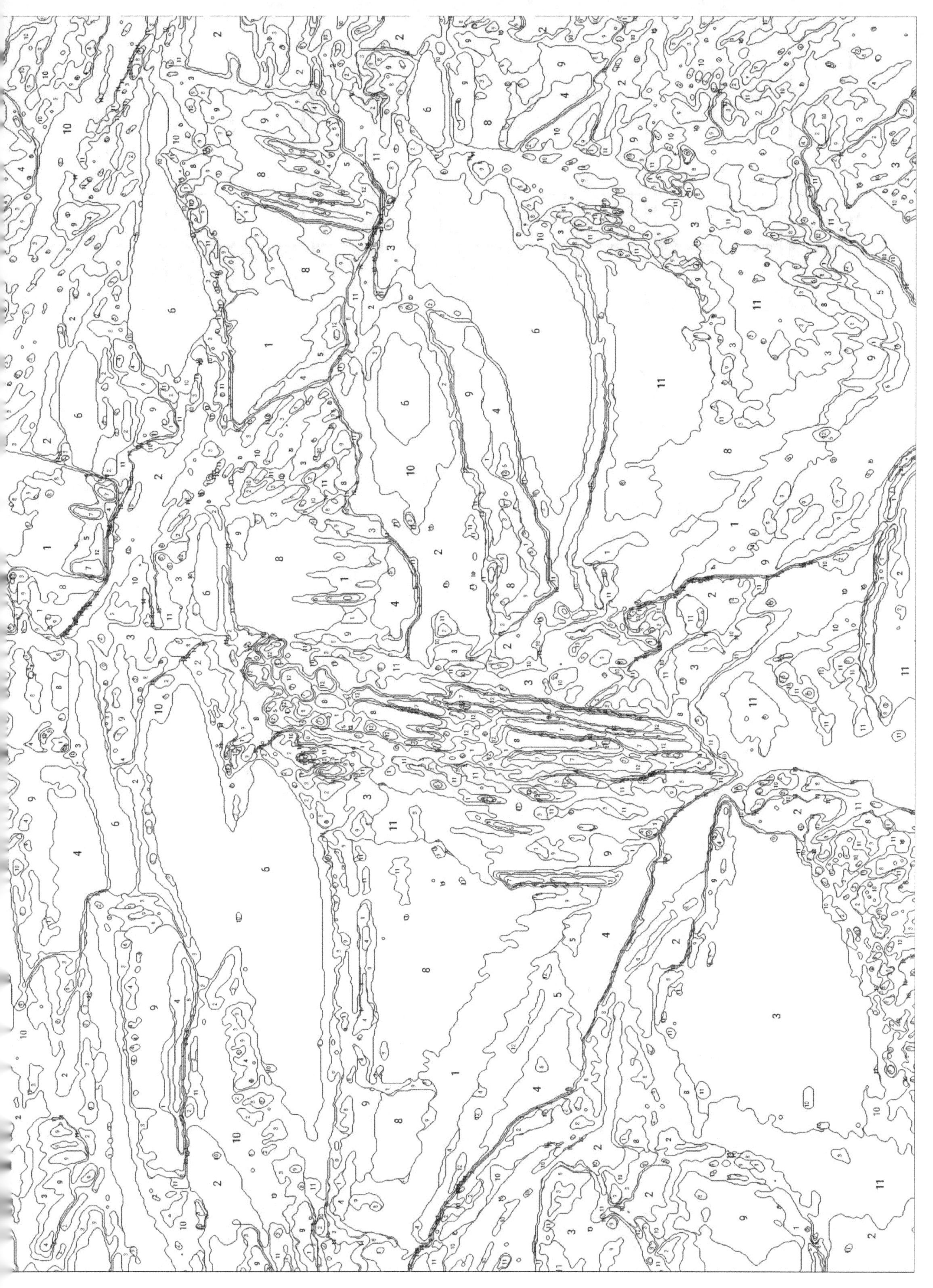

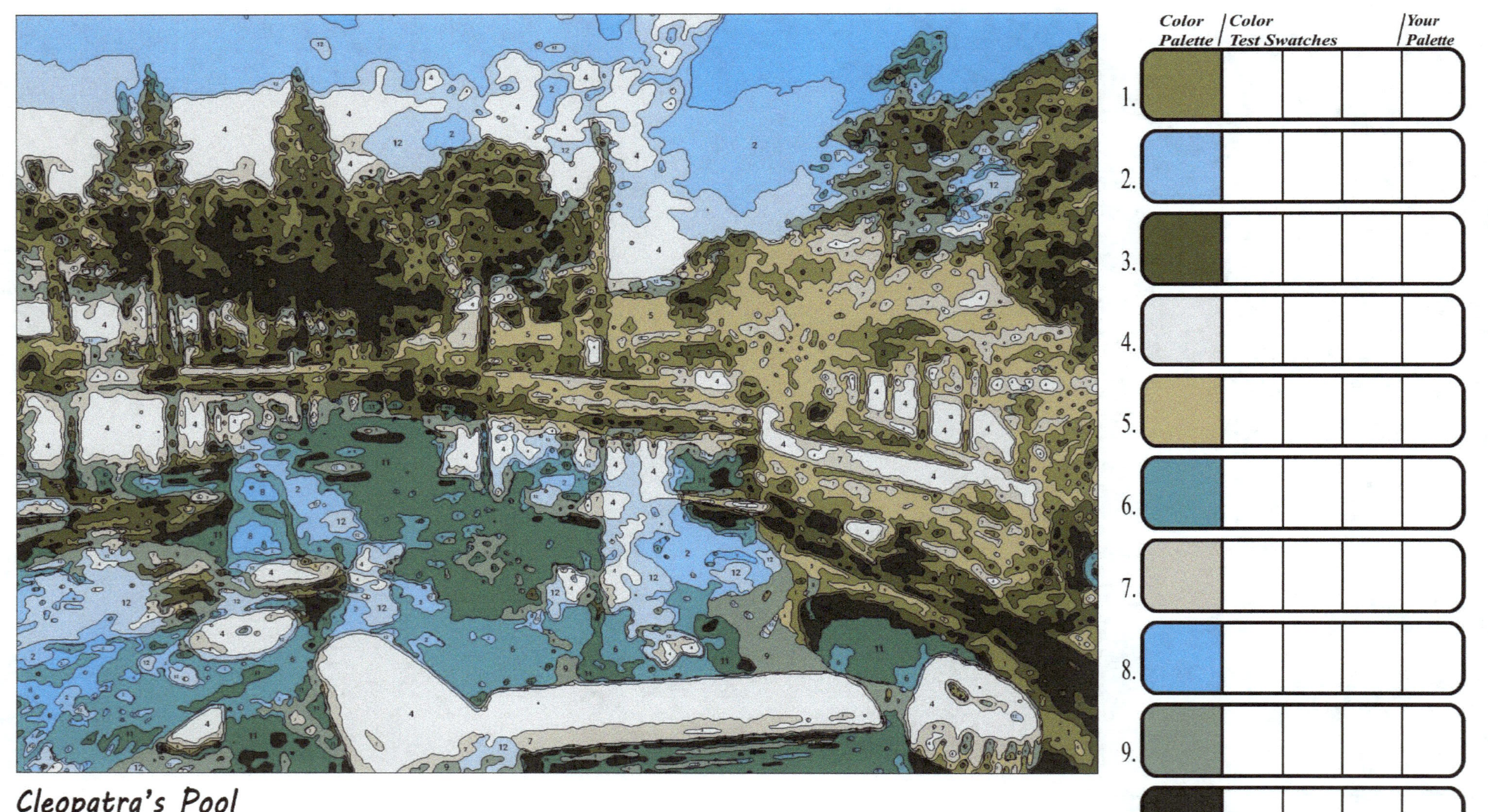

Color Palette	Color Test Swatches			Your Palette
1.				
2.				
3.				
4.				
5.				
6.				
7.				
8.				
9.				
10.				
11.				
12.				

Cleopatra's Pool

Cleopatra's Pool is a thermal pool with water temperatures of 36º-57ºC. This pool is within the Hierapolis site, in Pamukkale, Denizli. Hierapolis dates back to the 2nd century BC.

QR code Help File

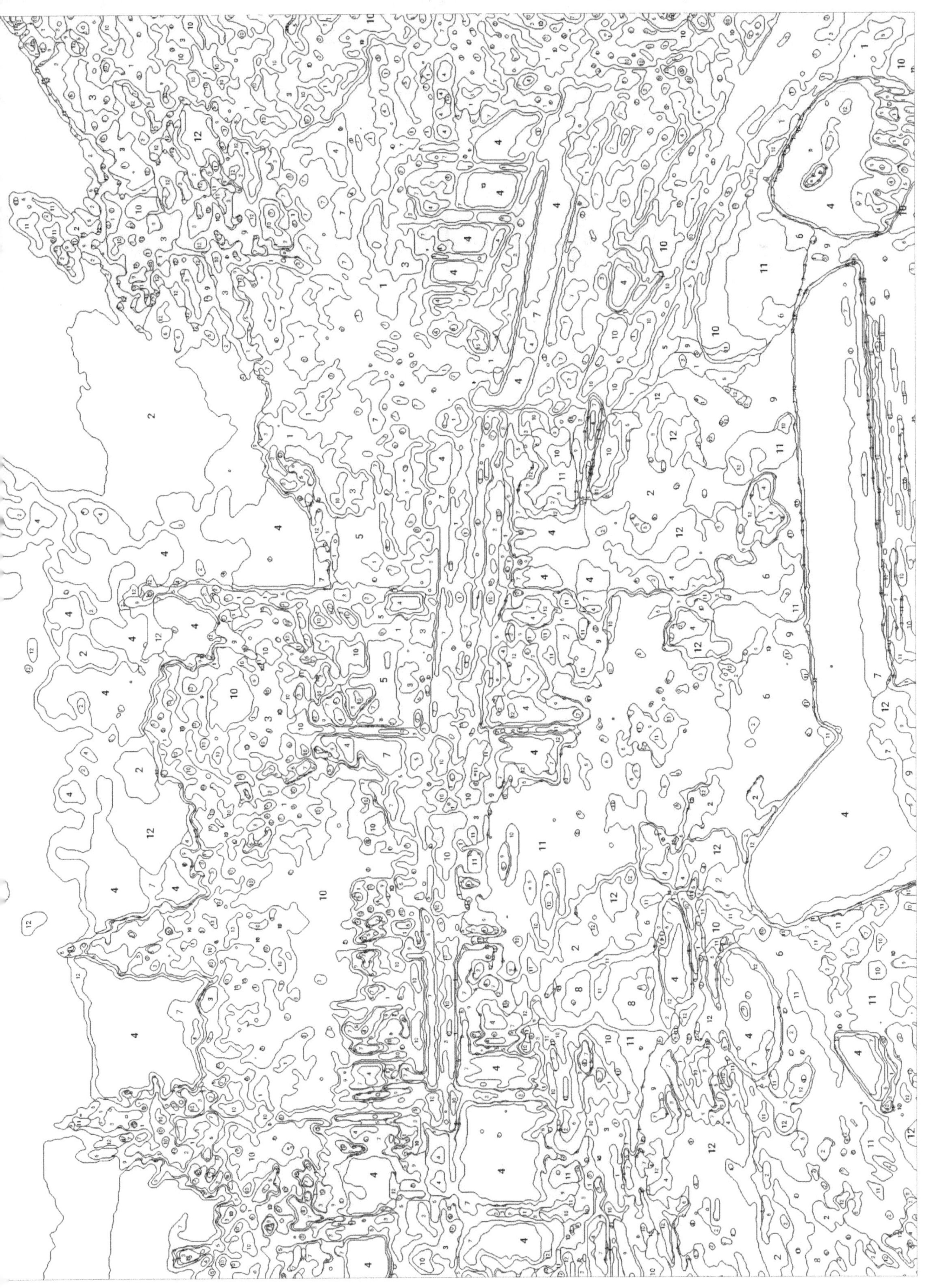

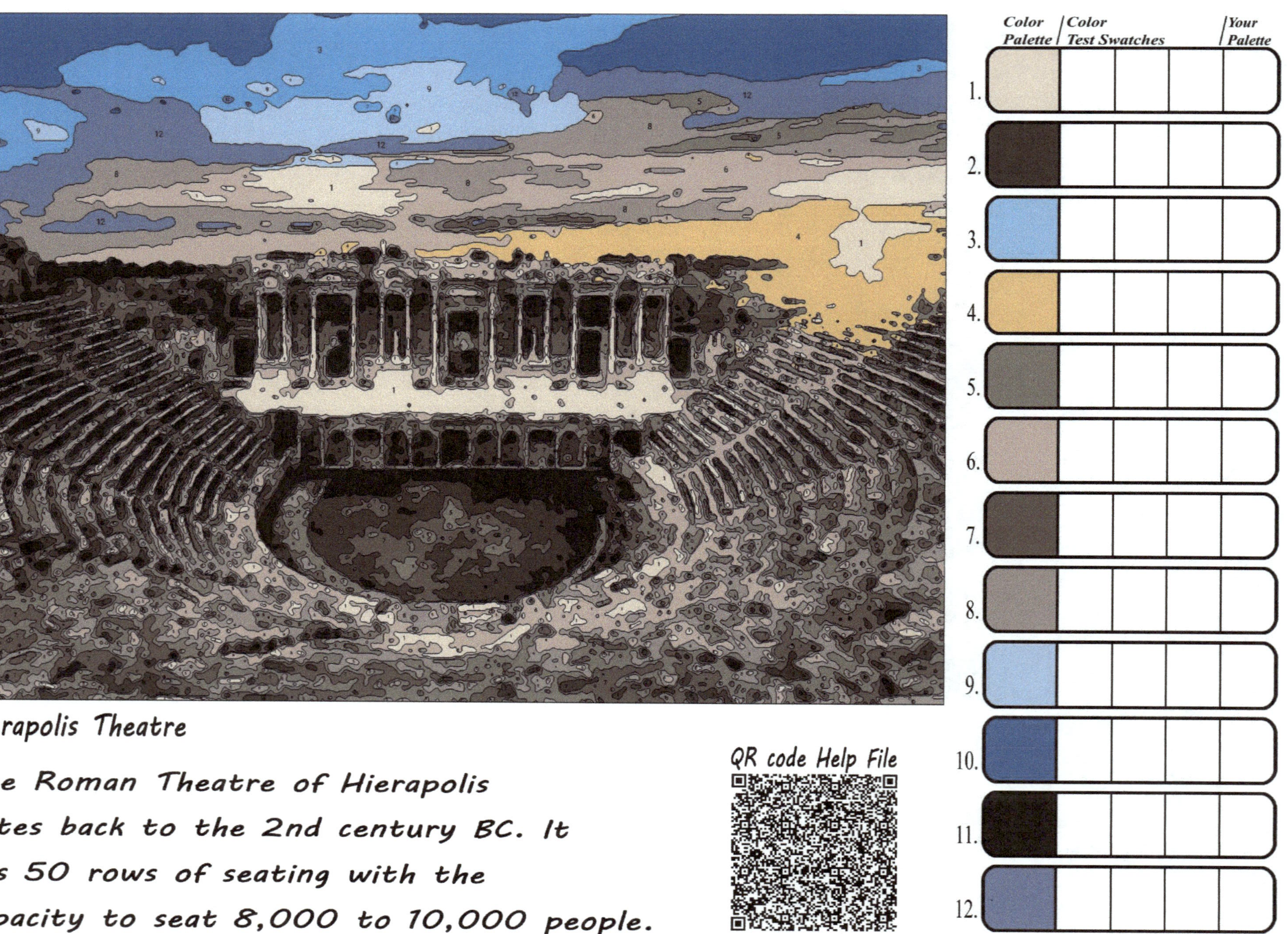

Hierapolis Theatre

The Roman Theatre of Hierapolis dates back to the 2nd century BC. It has 50 rows of seating with the capacity to seat 8,000 to 10,000 people.

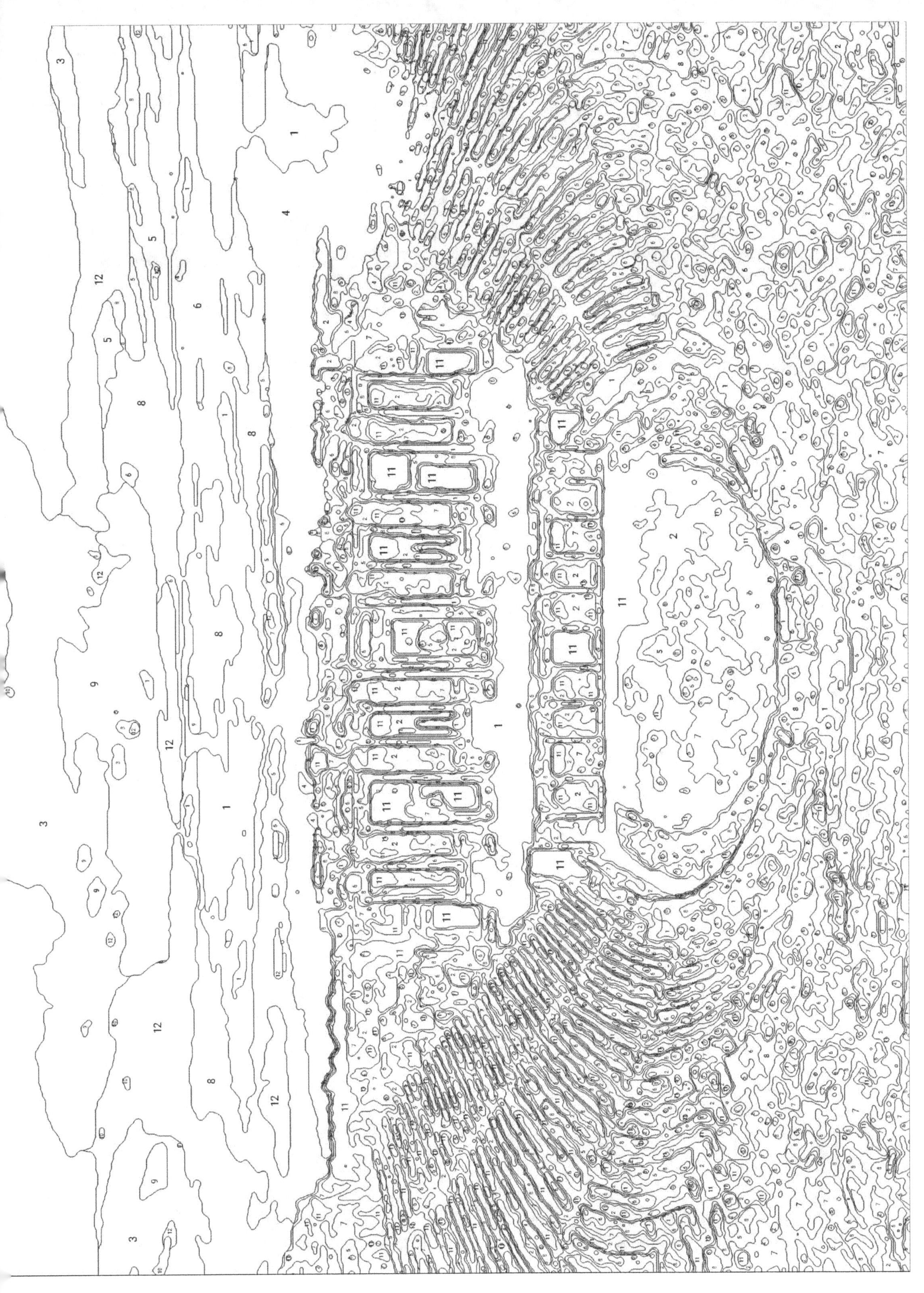

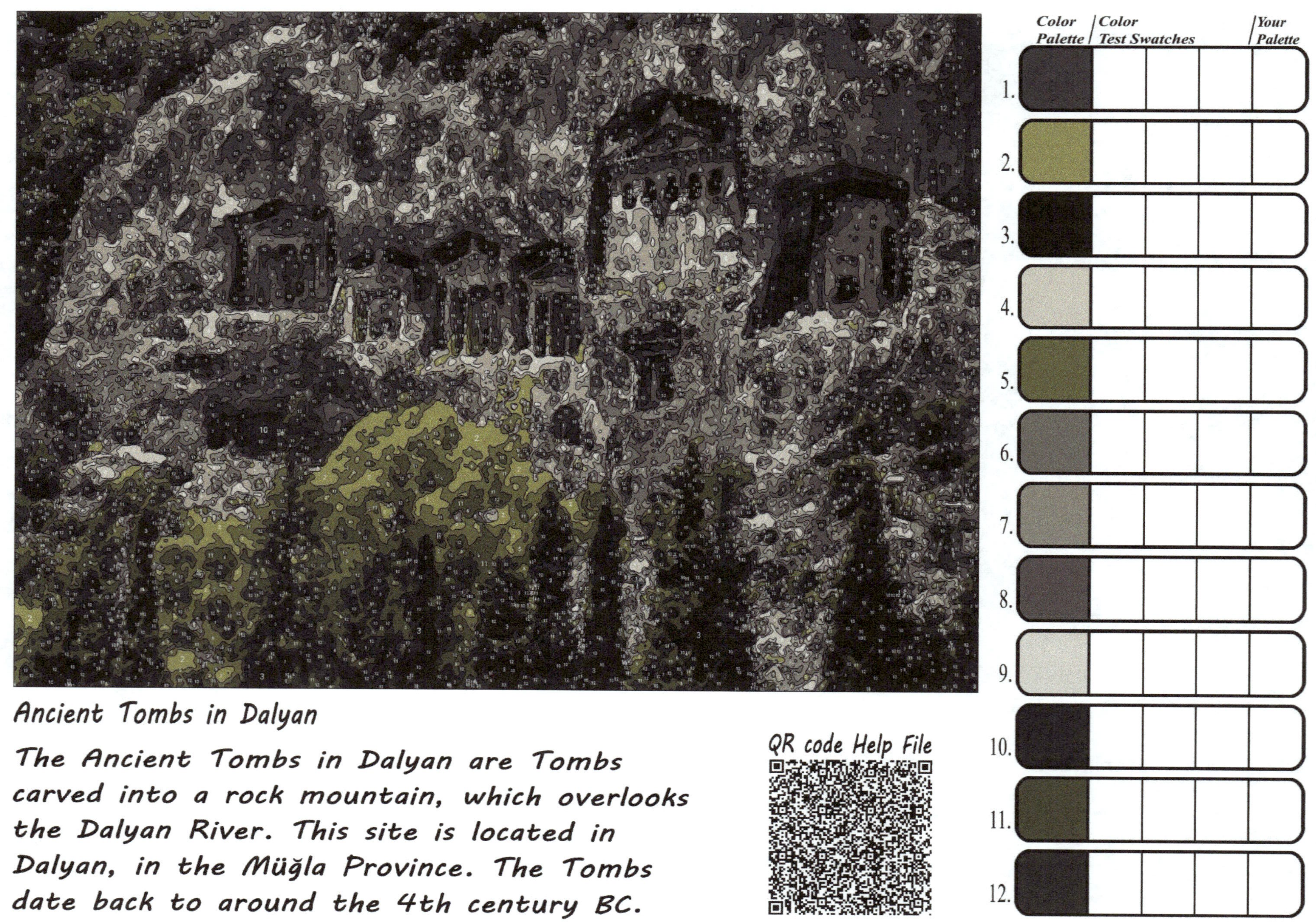

Ancient Tombs in Dalyan

The Ancient Tombs in Dalyan are Tombs carved into a rock mountain, which overlooks the Dalyan River. This site is located in Dalyan, in the Müğla Province. The Tombs date back to around the 4th century BC.

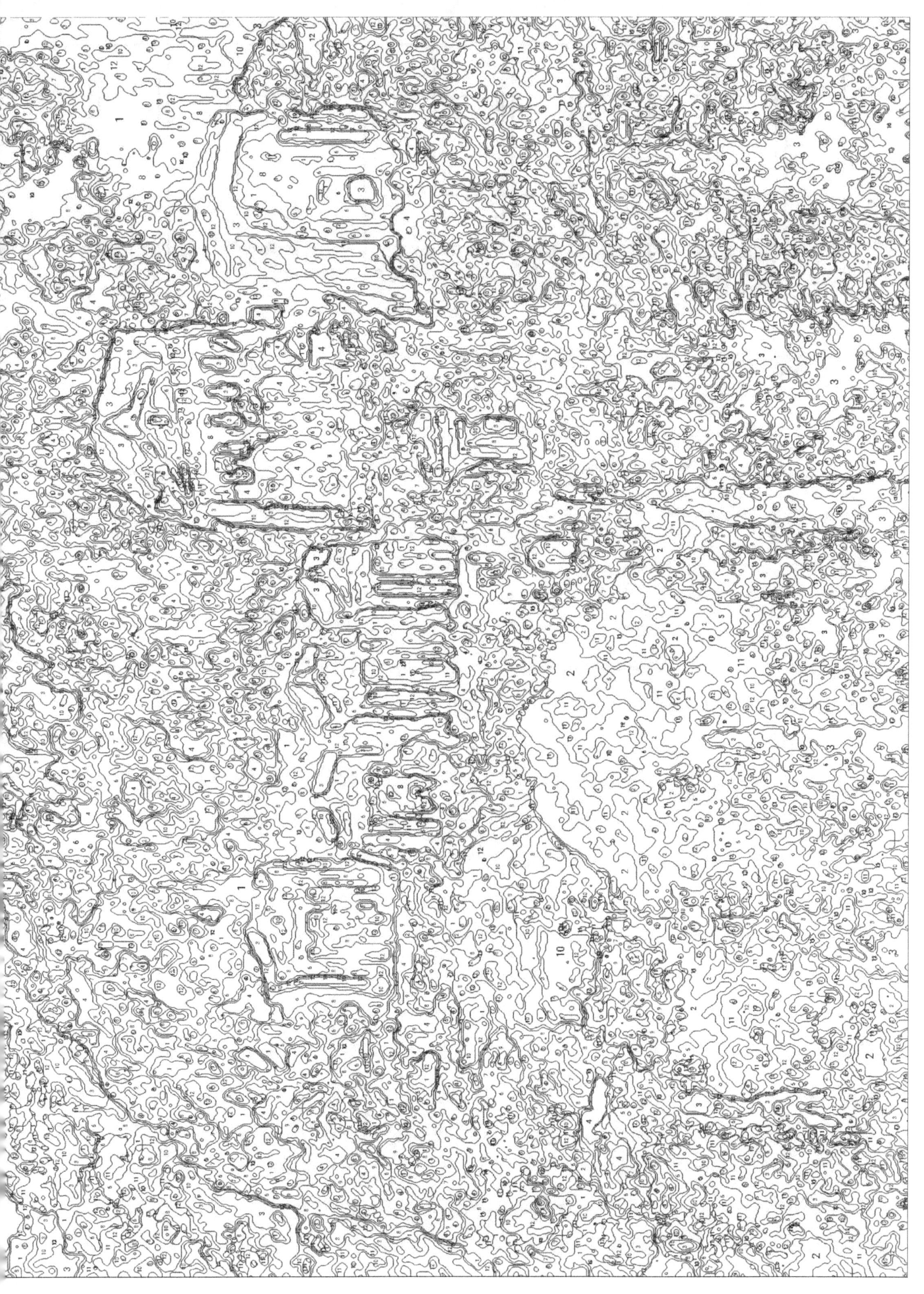

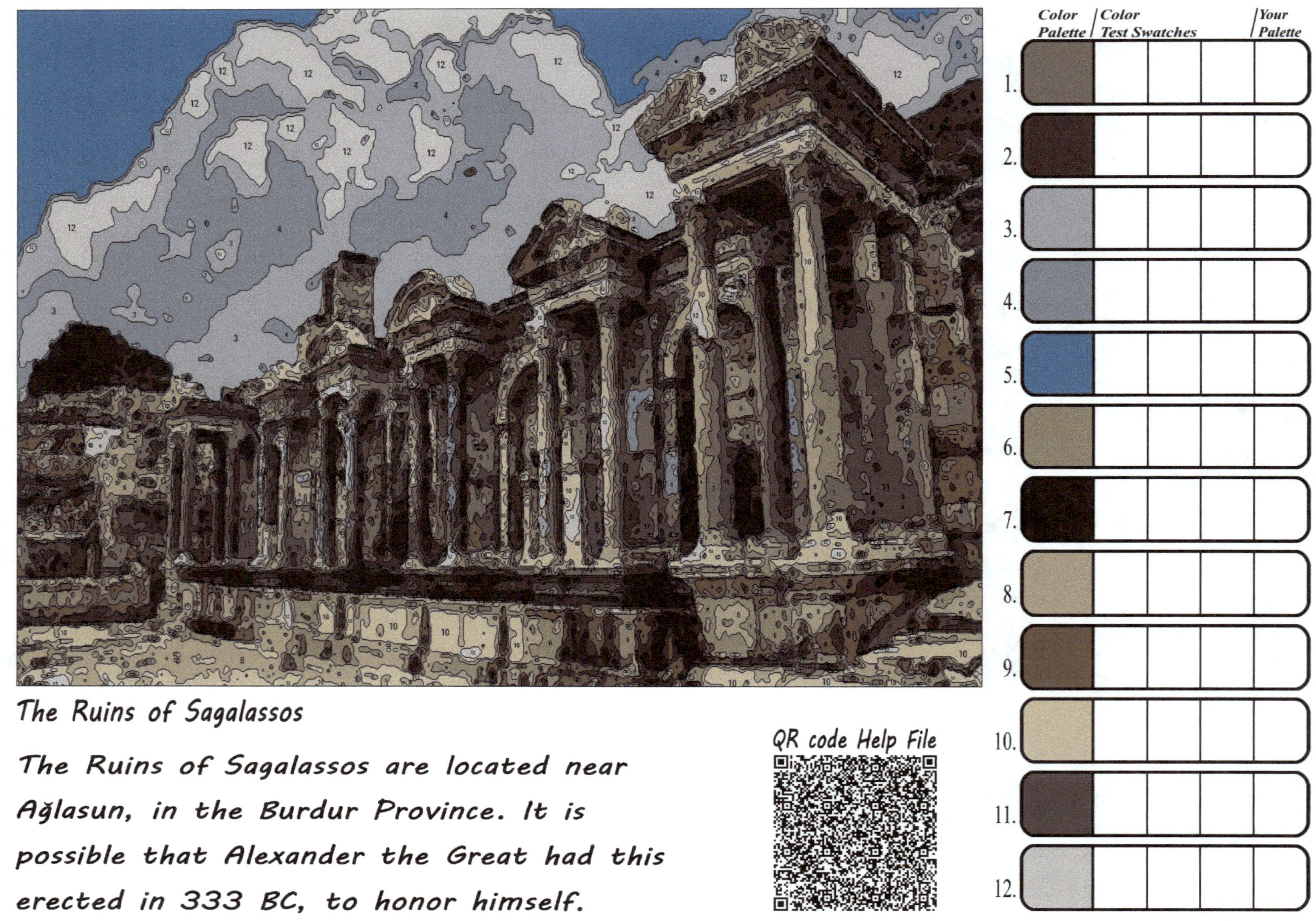

The Ruins of Sagalassos

The Ruins of Sagalassos are located near Ağlasun, in the Burdur Province. It is possible that Alexander the Great had this erected in 333 BC, to honor himself.

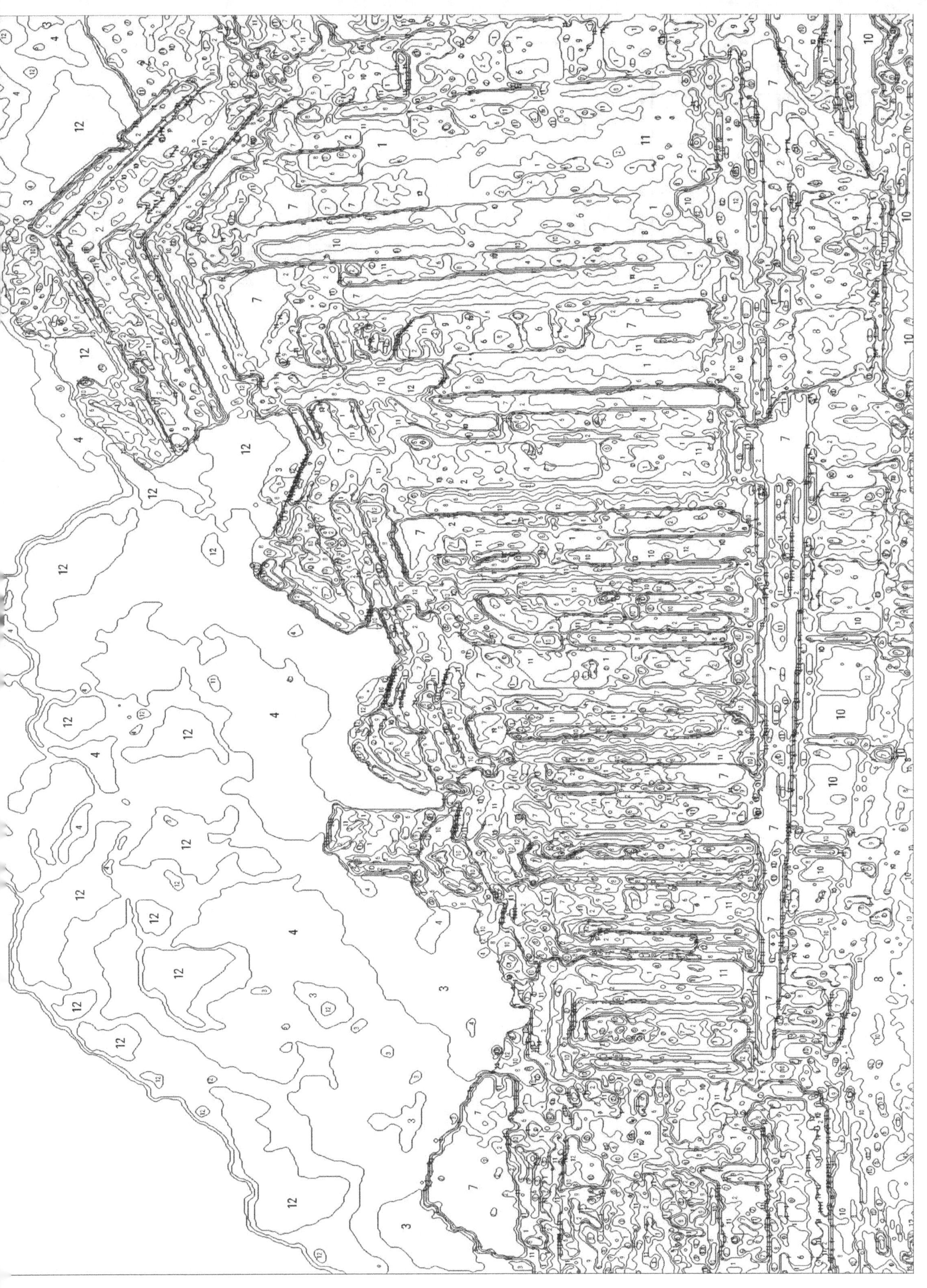

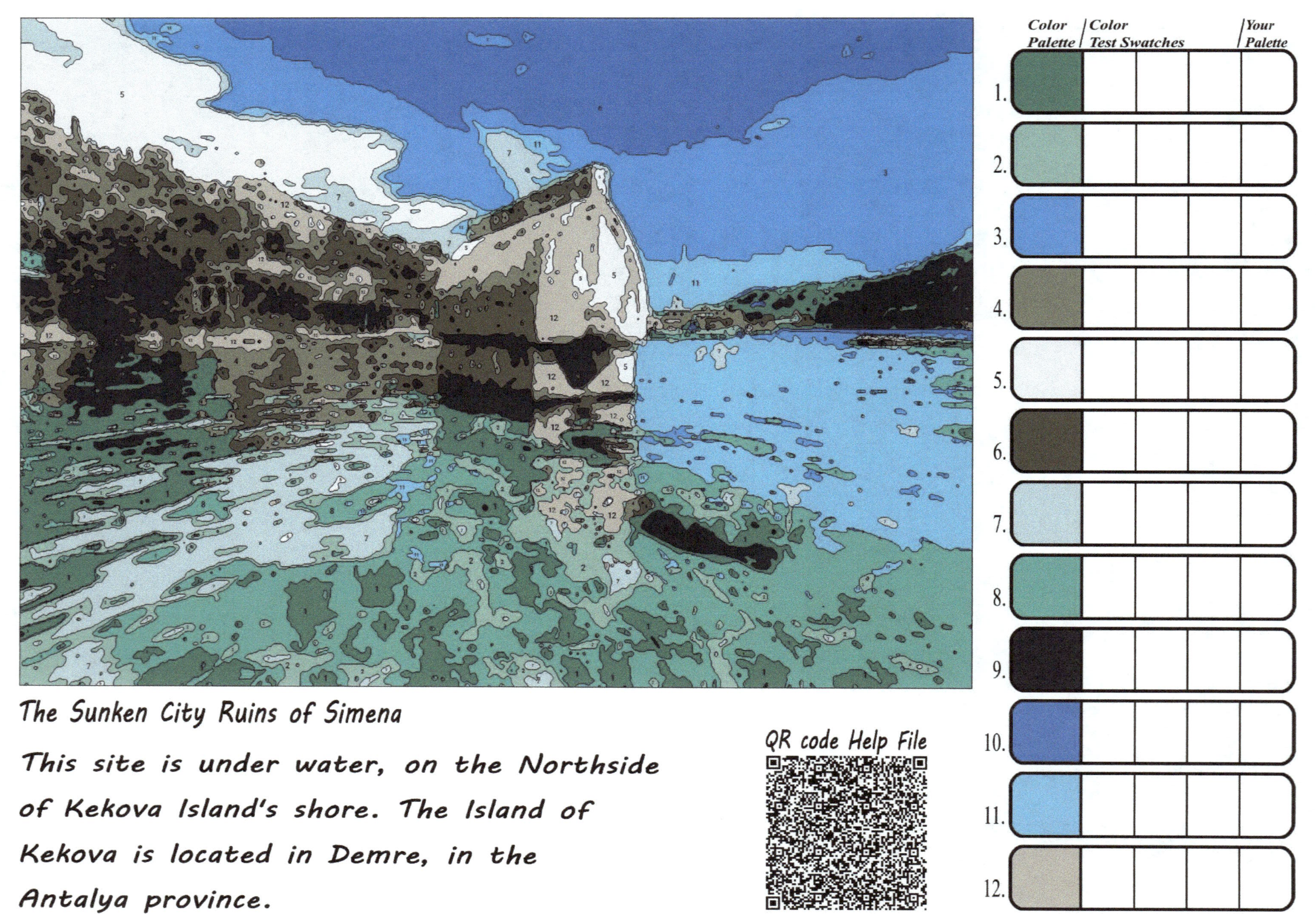

The Sunken City Ruins of Simena

This site is under water, on the Northside of Kekova Island's shore. The Island of Kekova is located in Demre, in the Antalya province.

QR code Help File

Color Palette	Color Test Swatches				Your Palette
1.					
2.					
3.					
4.					
5.					
6.					
7.					
8.					
9.					
10.					
11.					
12.					

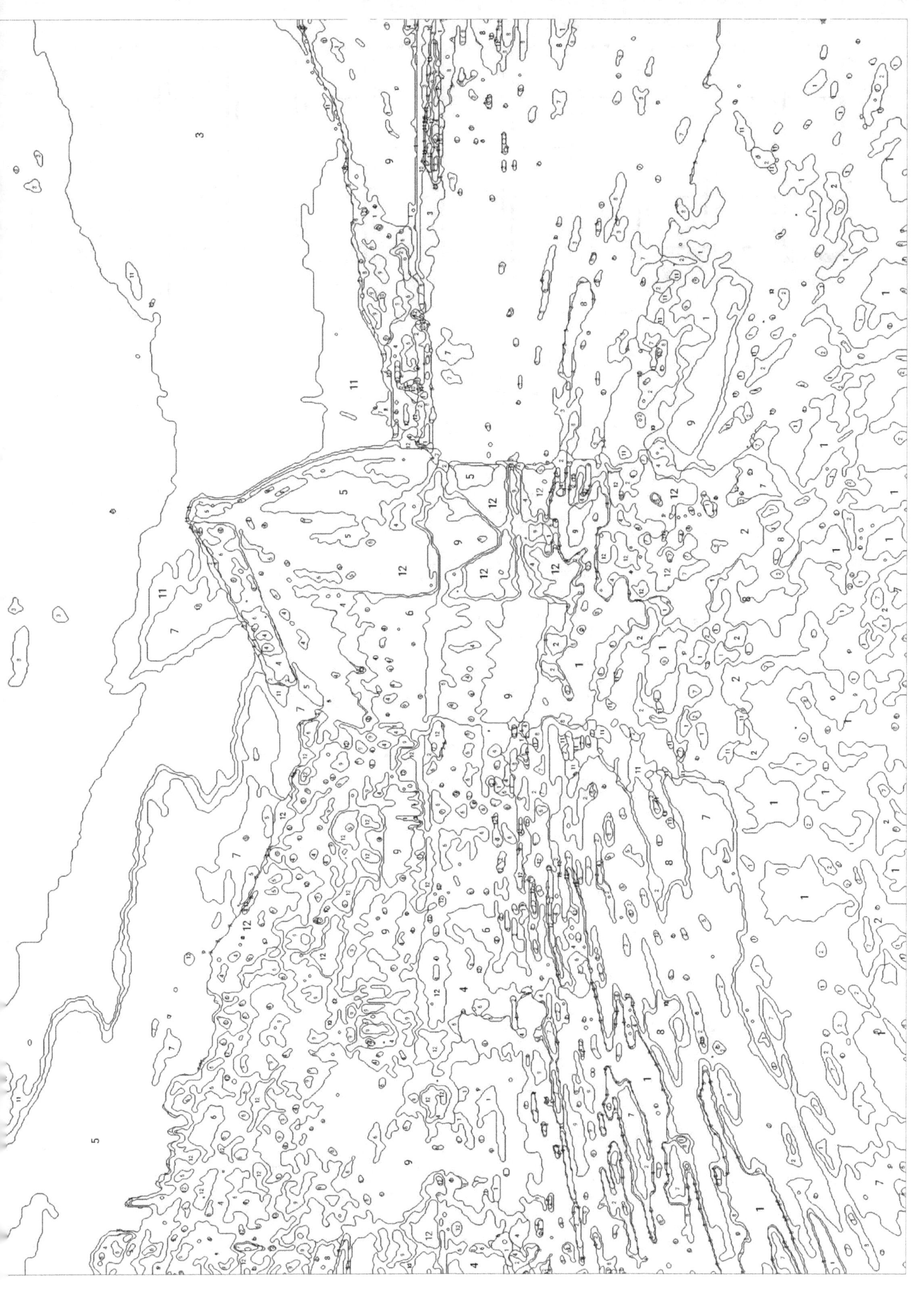

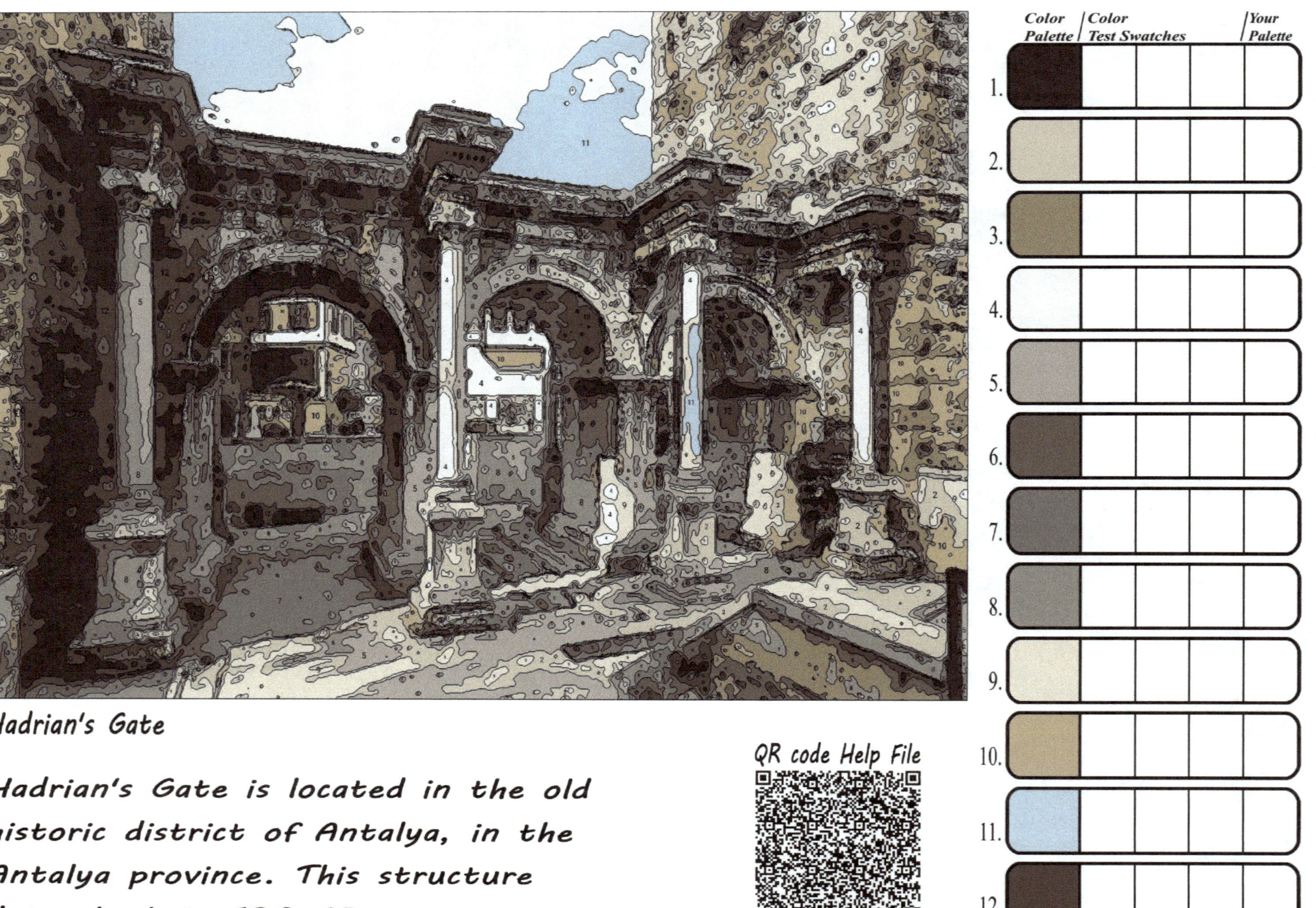

Hadrian's Gate

Hadrian's Gate is located in the old historic district of Antalya, in the Antalya province. This structure dates back to 130 AD.

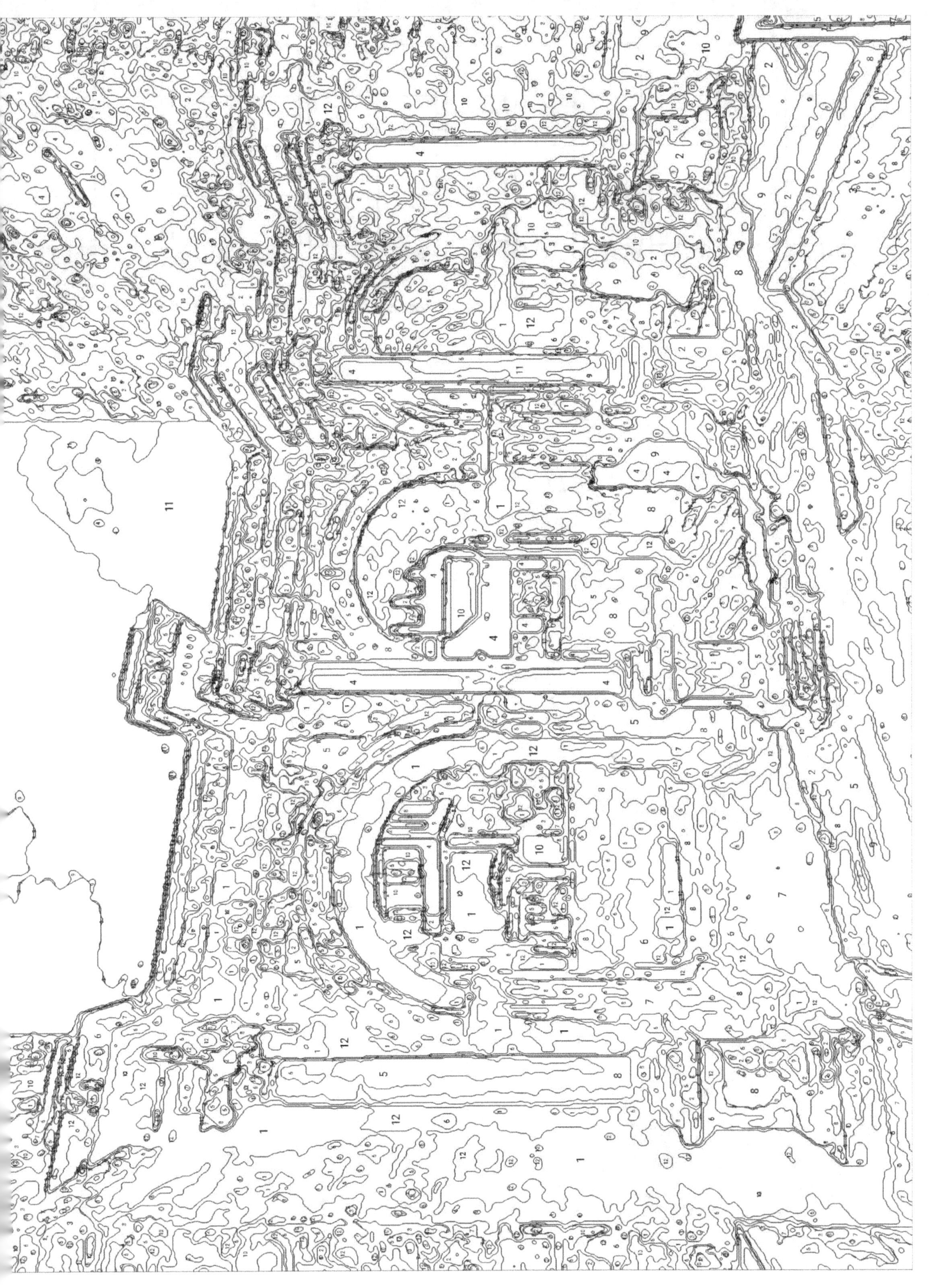

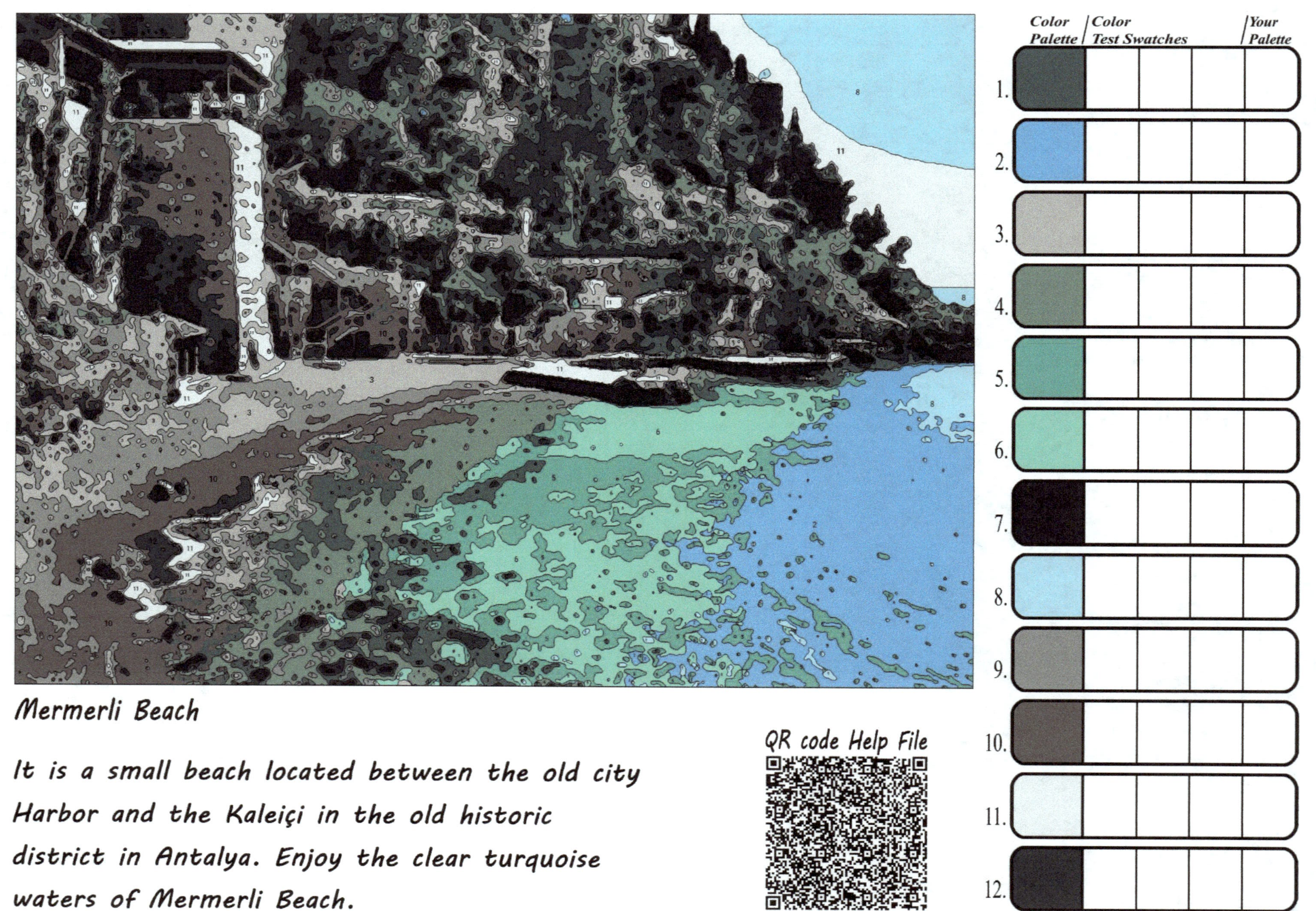

Mermerli Beach

It is a small beach located between the old city Harbor and the Kaleiçi in the old historic district in Antalya. Enjoy the clear turquoise waters of Mermerli Beach.

QR code Help File

	Color Palette	Color Test Swatches			Your Palette
1.					
2.					
3.					
4.					
5.					
6.					
7.					
8.					
9.					
10.					
11.					
12.					

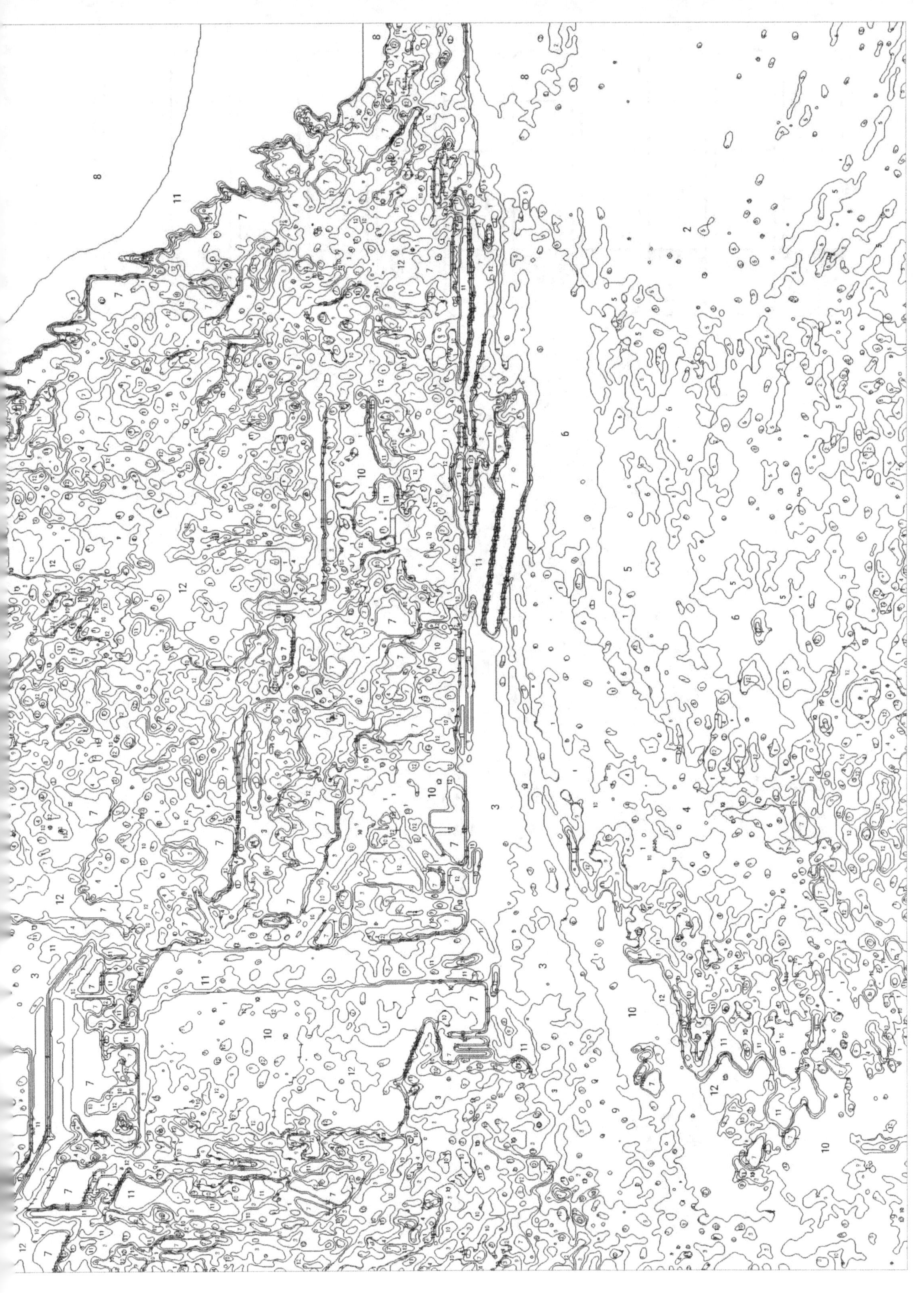

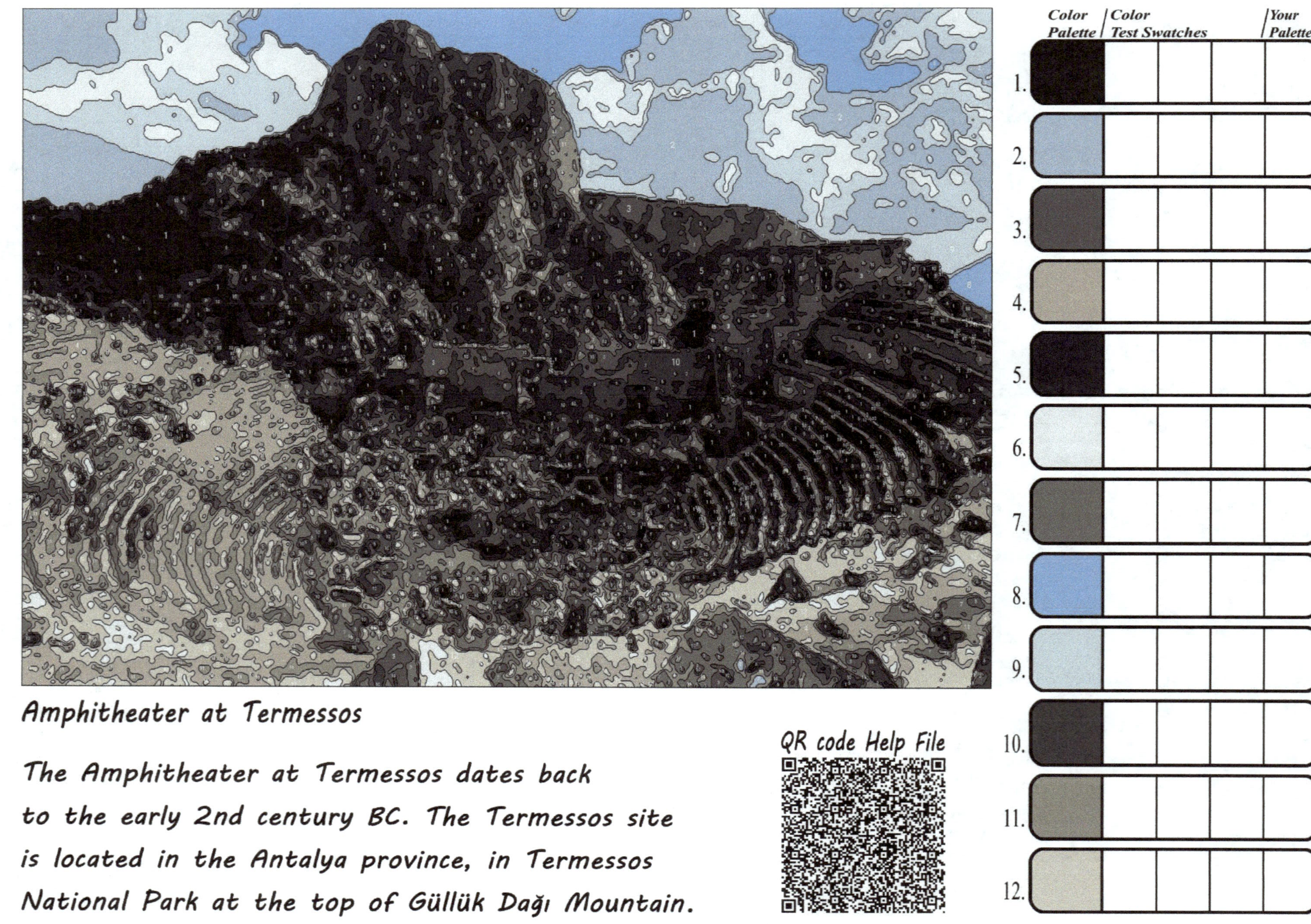

	Color Palette	Color Test Swatches			Your Palette
1.					
2.					
3.					
4.					
5.					
6.					
7.					
8.					
9.					
10.					
11.					
12.					

Amphitheater at Termessos

The Amphitheater at Termessos dates back to the early 2nd century BC. The Termessos site is located in the Antalya province, in Termessos National Park at the top of Güllük Dağı Mountain.

QR code Help File

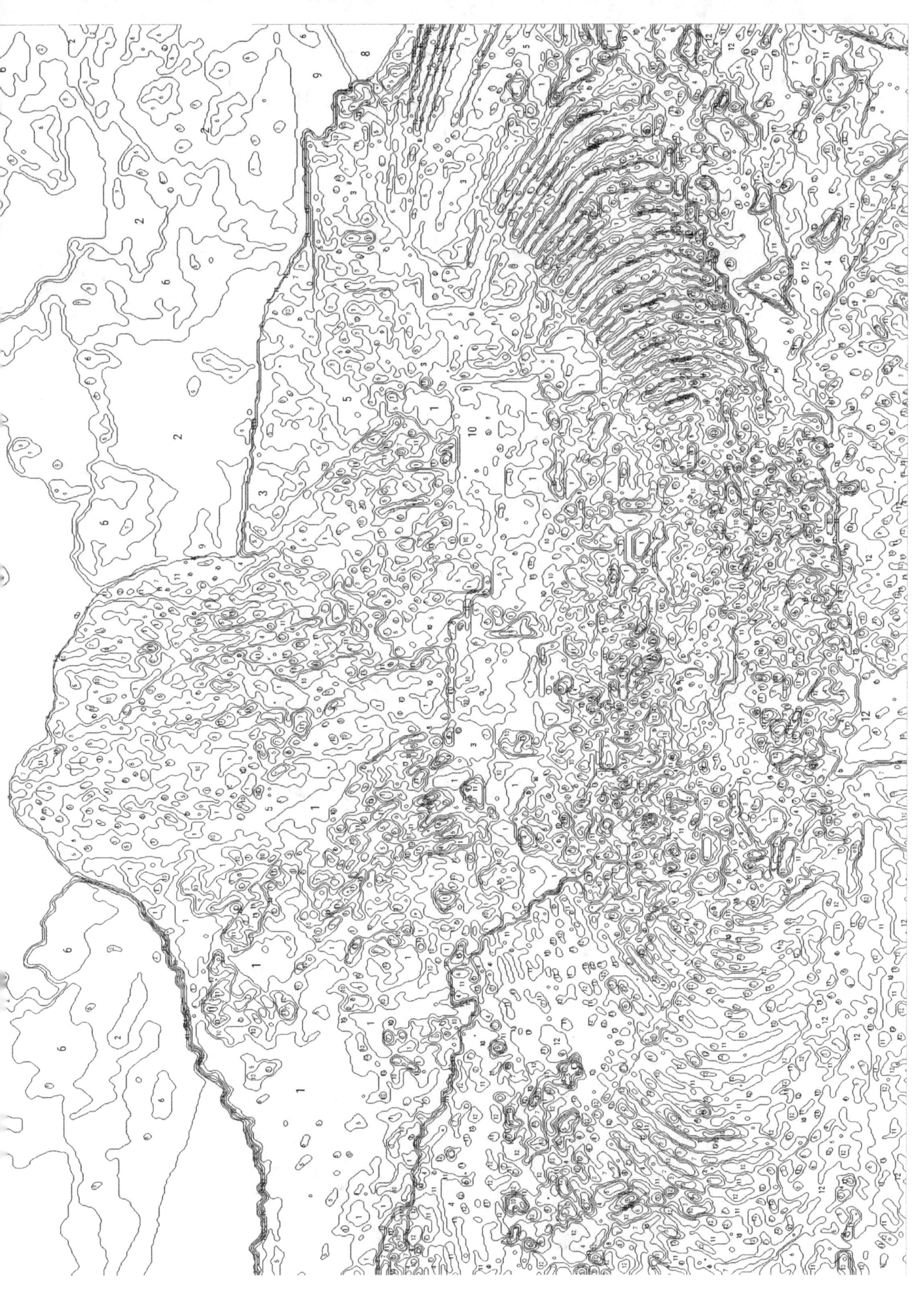

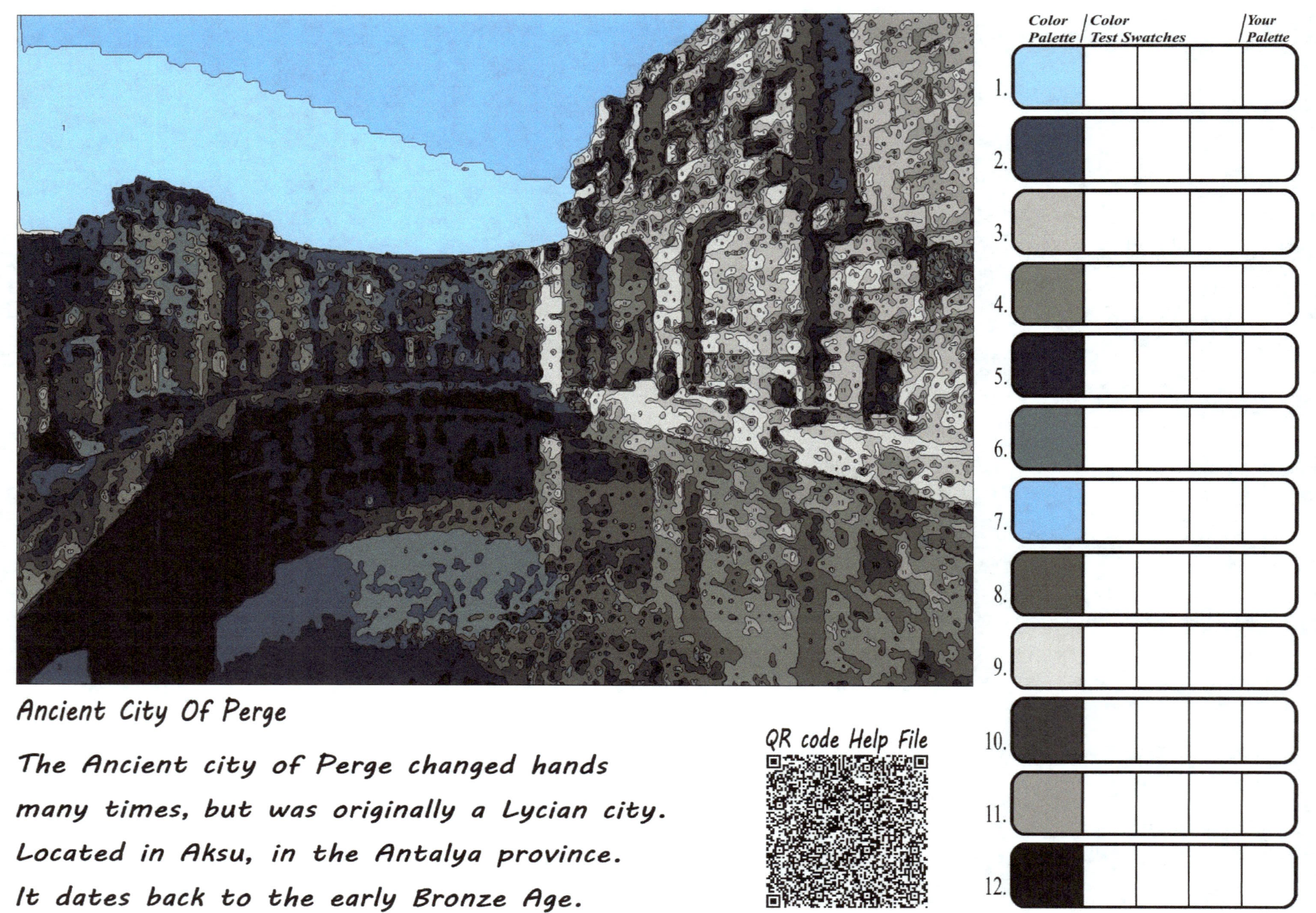

Ancient City Of Perge

The Ancient city of Perge changed hands many times, but was originally a Lycian city. Located in Aksu, in the Antalya province. It dates back to the early Bronze Age.

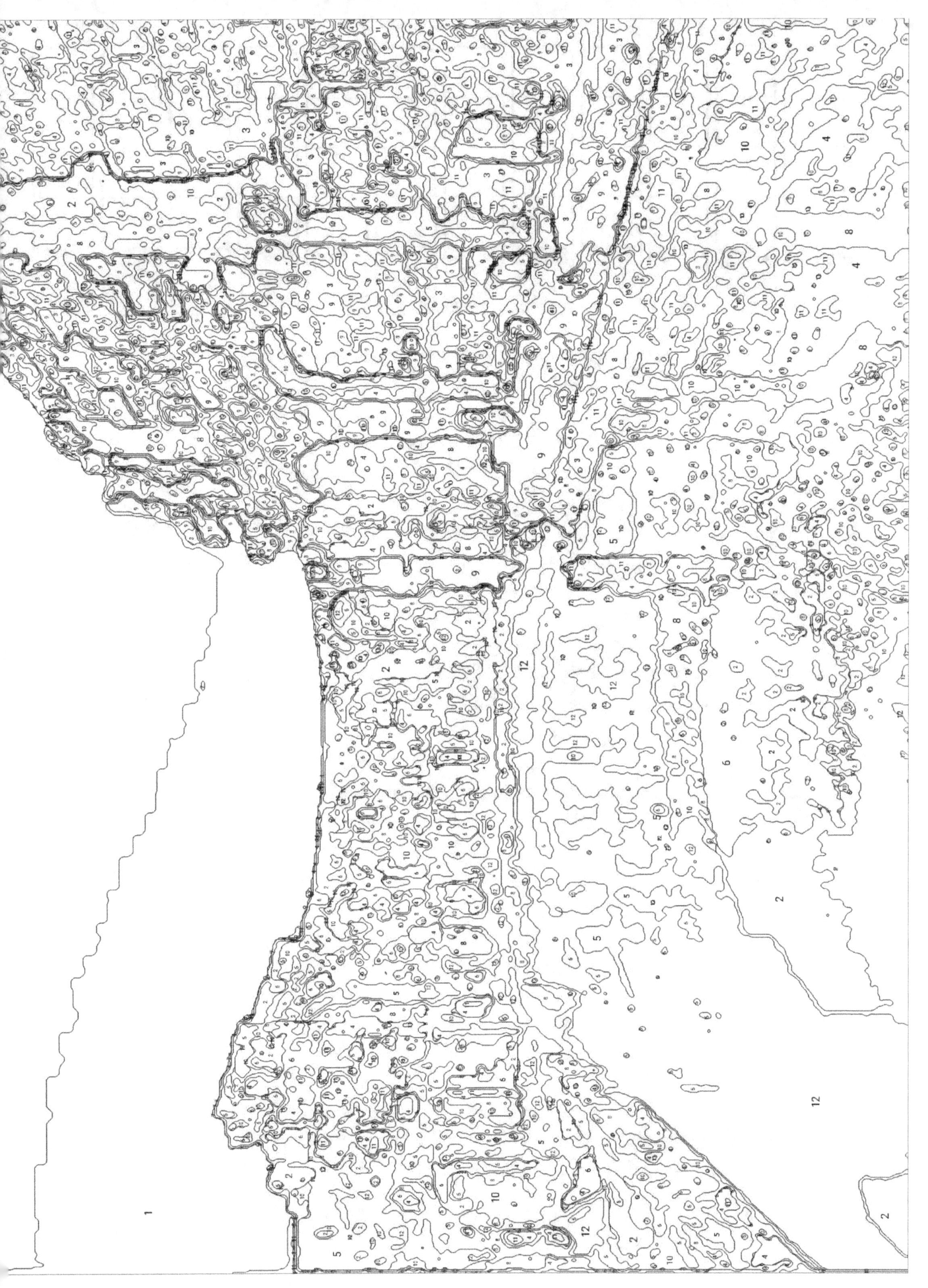

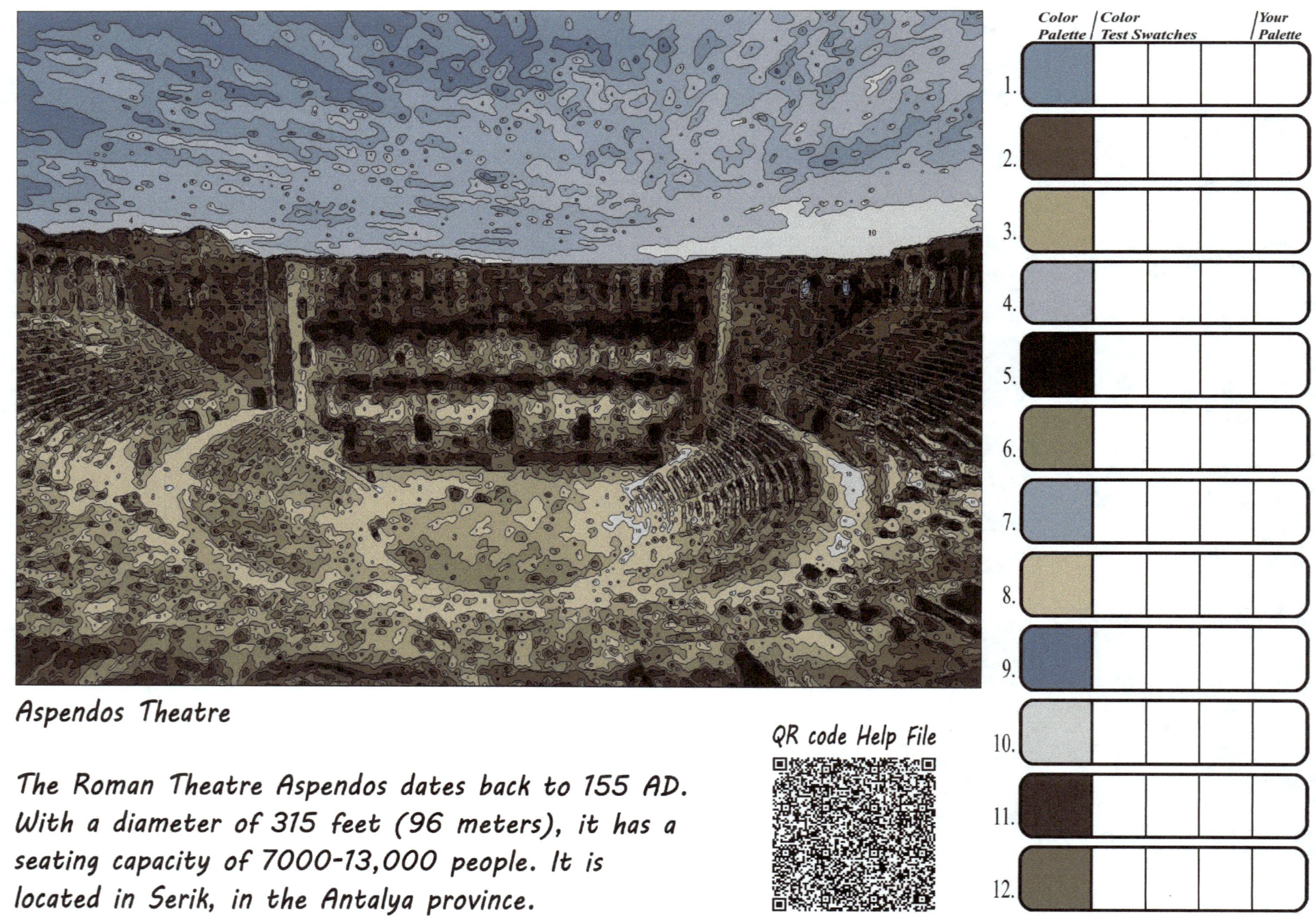

Aspendos Theatre

The Roman Theatre Aspendos dates back to 155 AD. With a diameter of 315 feet (96 meters), it has a seating capacity of 7000-13,000 people. It is located in Serik, in the Antalya province.

QR code Help File

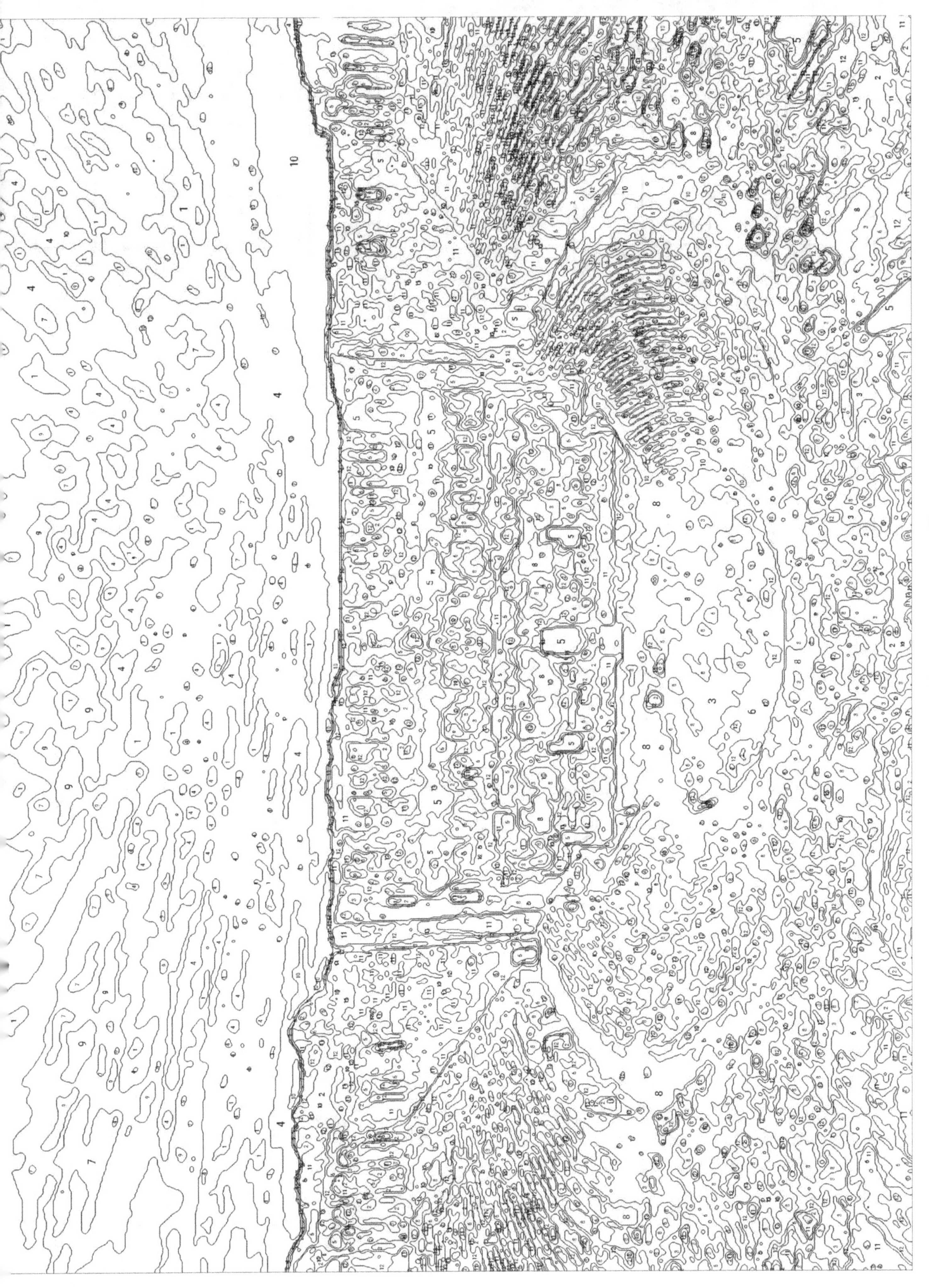

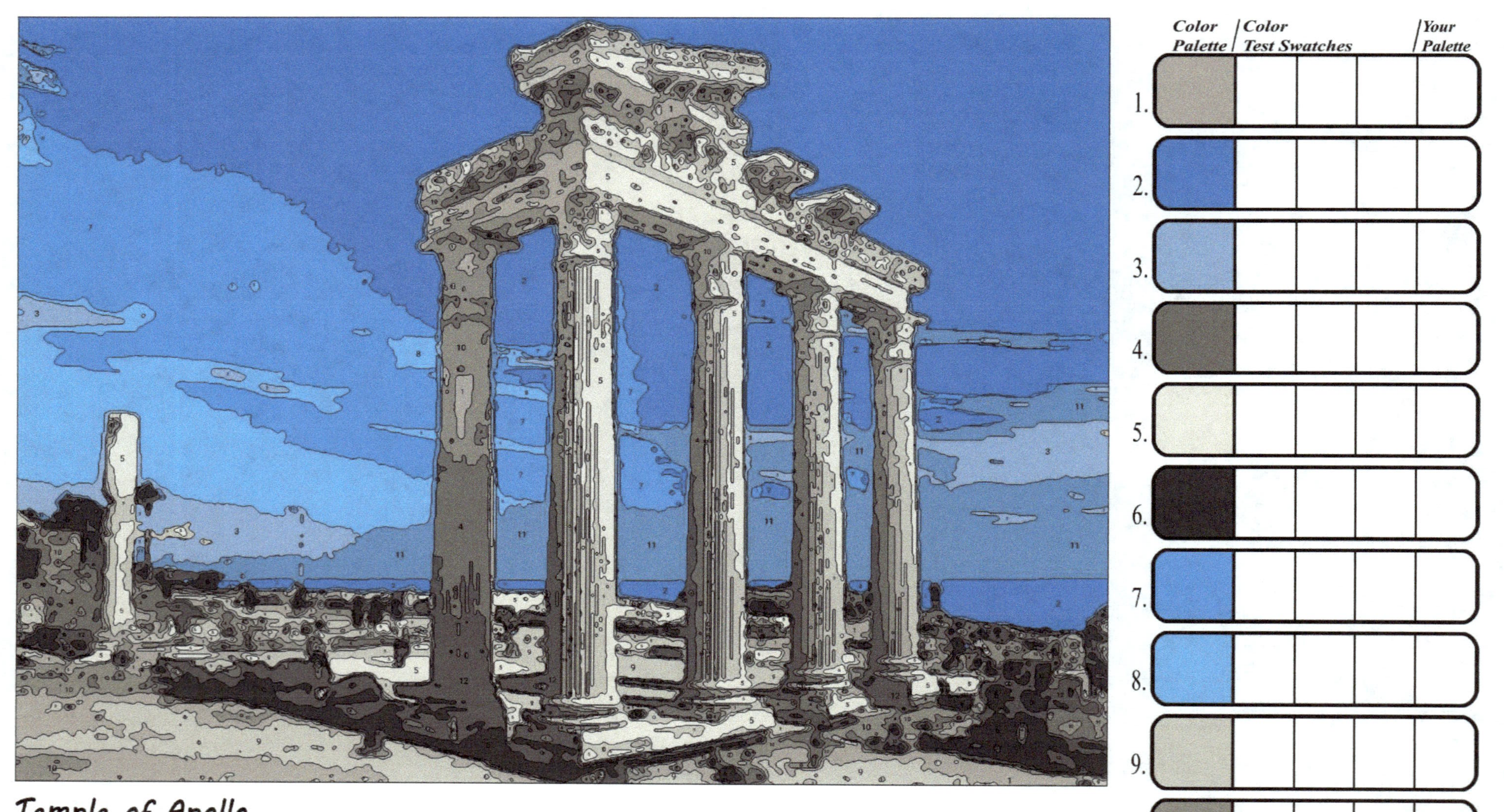

Temple of Apollo

The Roman Temple of Apollo dates back to 159 AD. It is a dedication to the Greek deity Apollo. It is located in Side, Antalya. It has a beautiful overlooking view of the Mediterranean Sea.

QR code Help File

Color Palette	Color Test Swatches			Your Palette
1.				
2.				
3.				
4.				
5.				
6.				
7.				
8.				
9.				
10.				
11.				
12.				

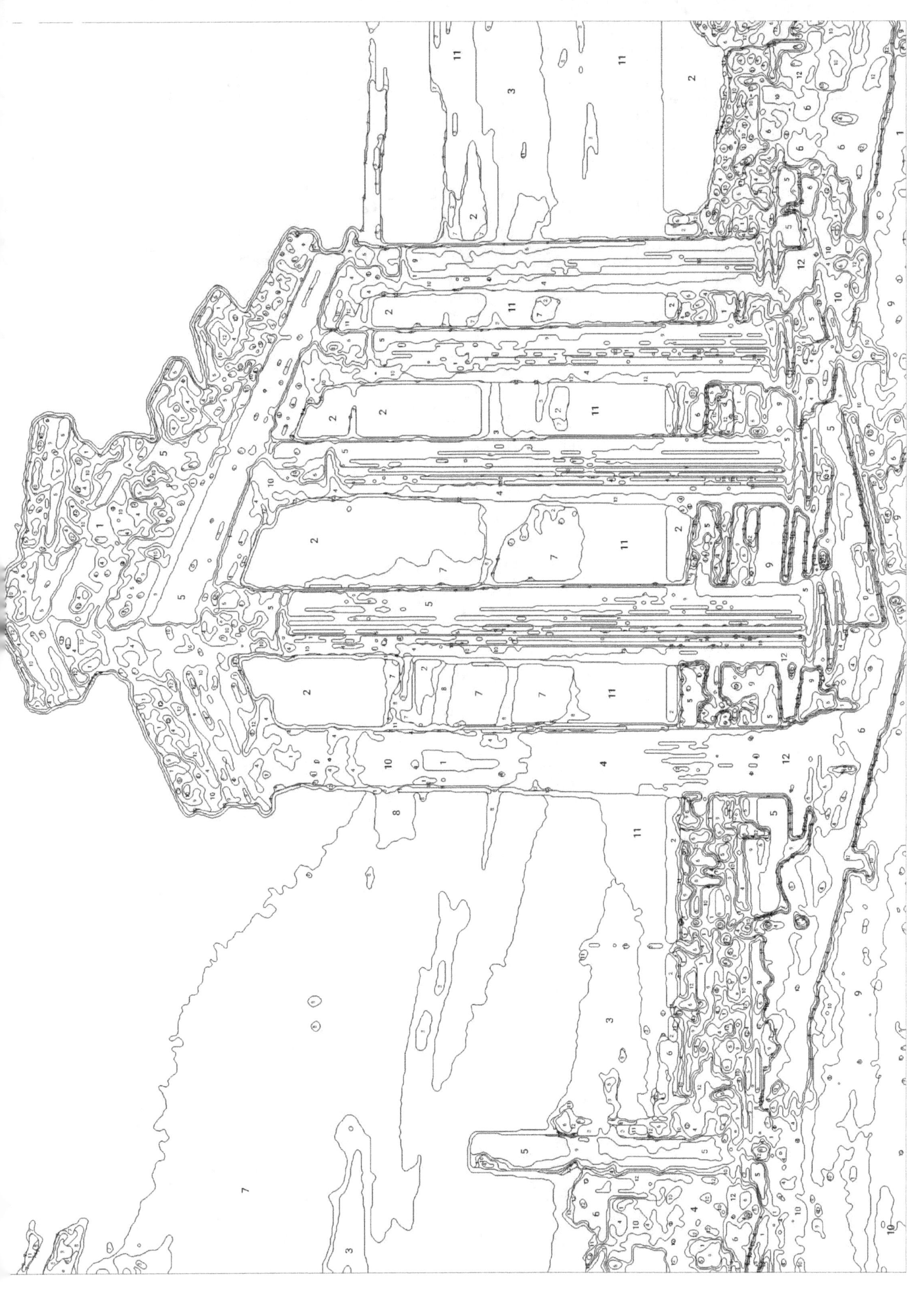

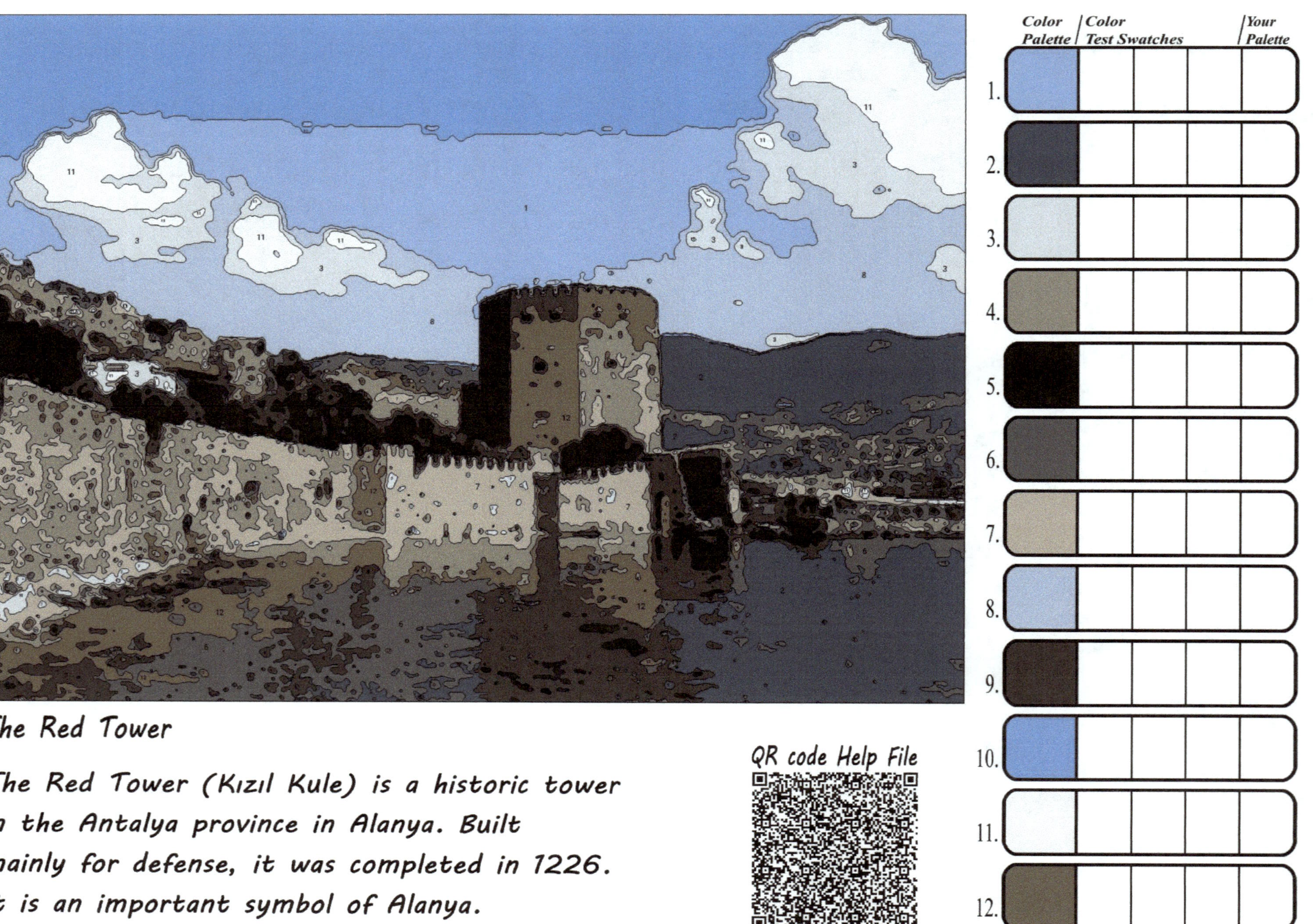

The Red Tower

The Red Tower (Kızıl Kule) is a historic tower in the Antalya province in Alanya. Built mainly for defense, it was completed in 1226. It is an important symbol of Alanya.

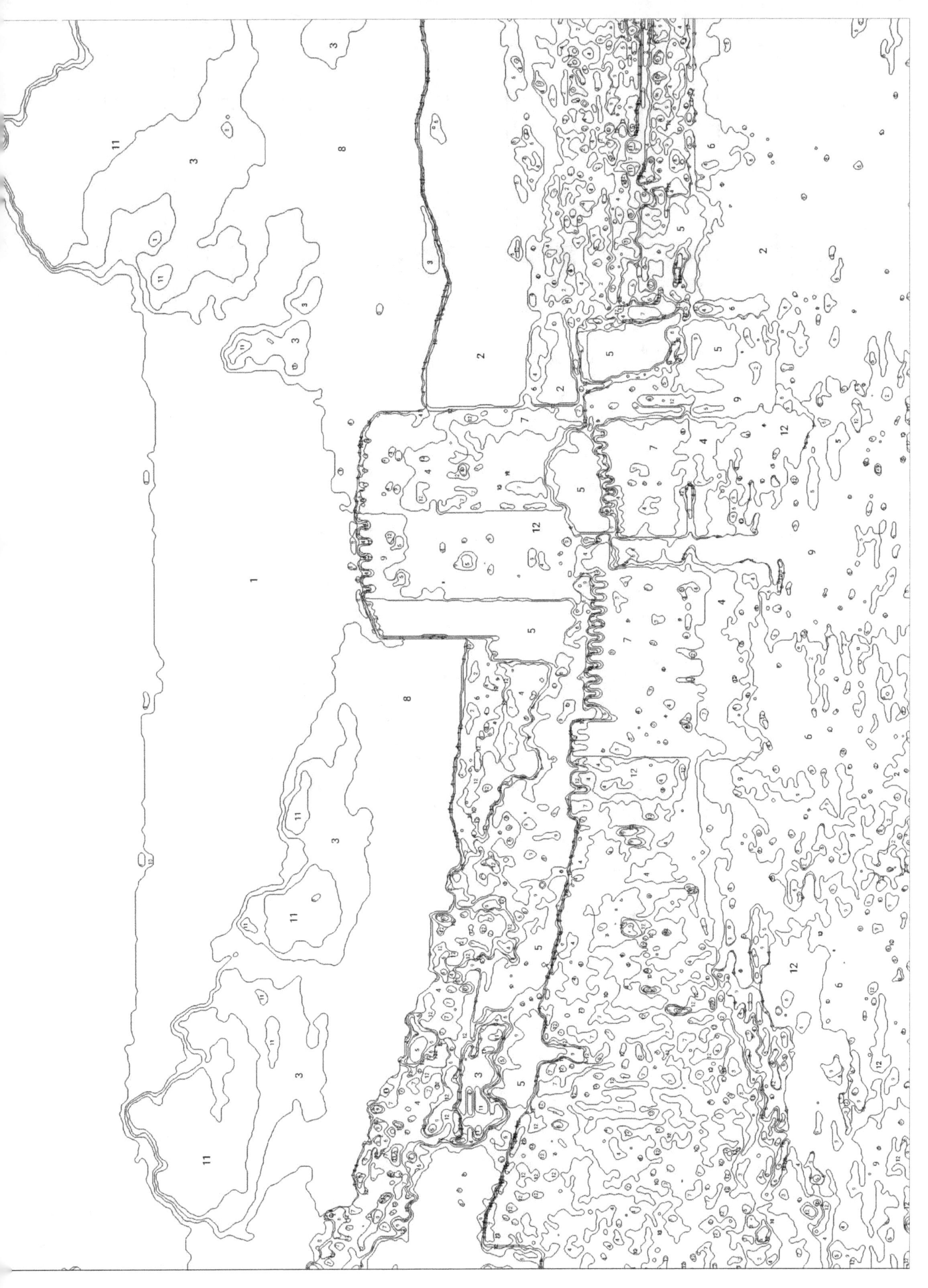

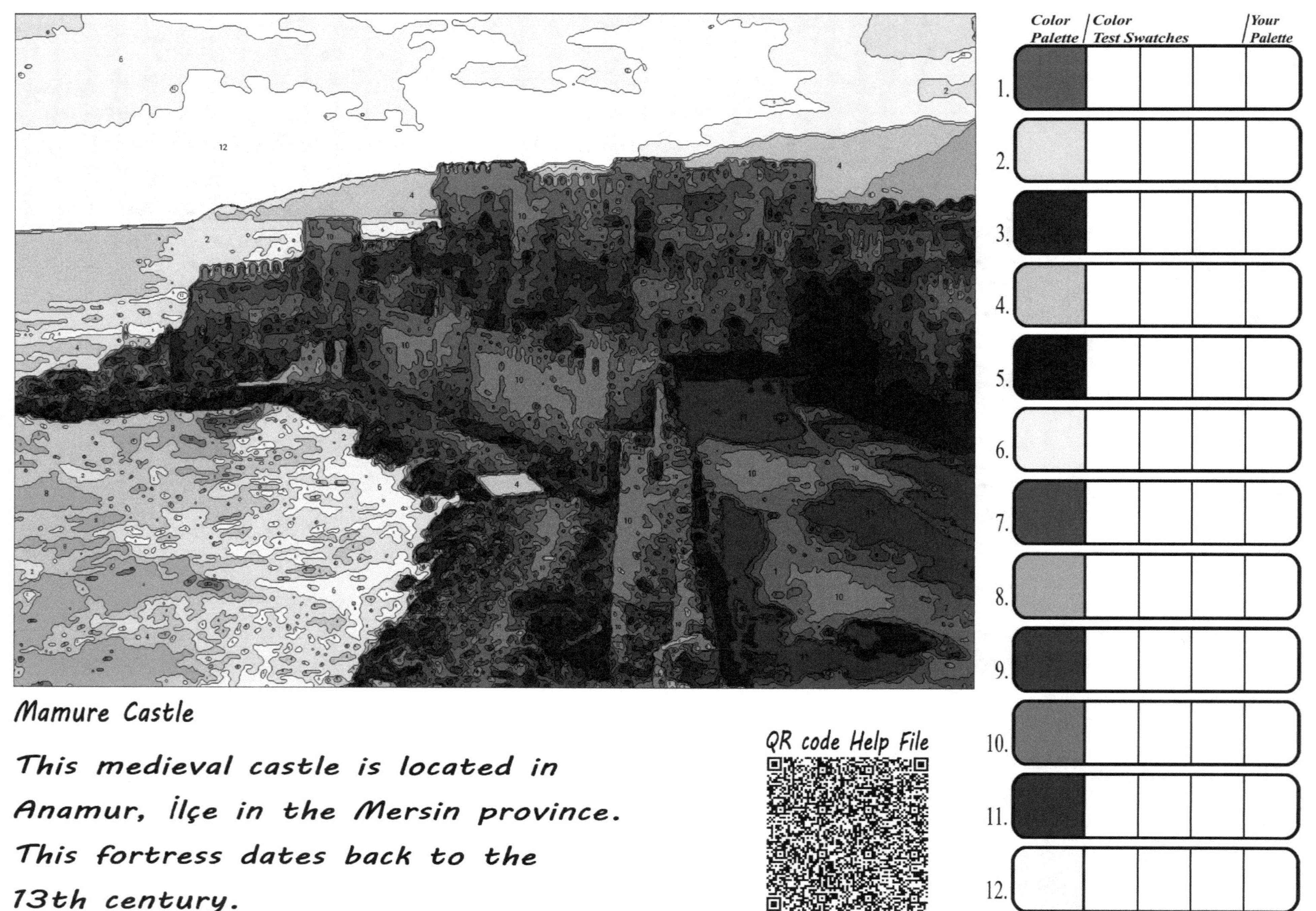

Mamure Castle

This medieval castle is located in Anamur, İlçe in the Mersin province. This fortress dates back to the 13th century.

QR code Help File

Color Palette	Color Test Swatches			Your Palette
1.				
2.				
3.				
4.				
5.				
6.				
7.				
8.				
9.				
10.				
11.				
12.				

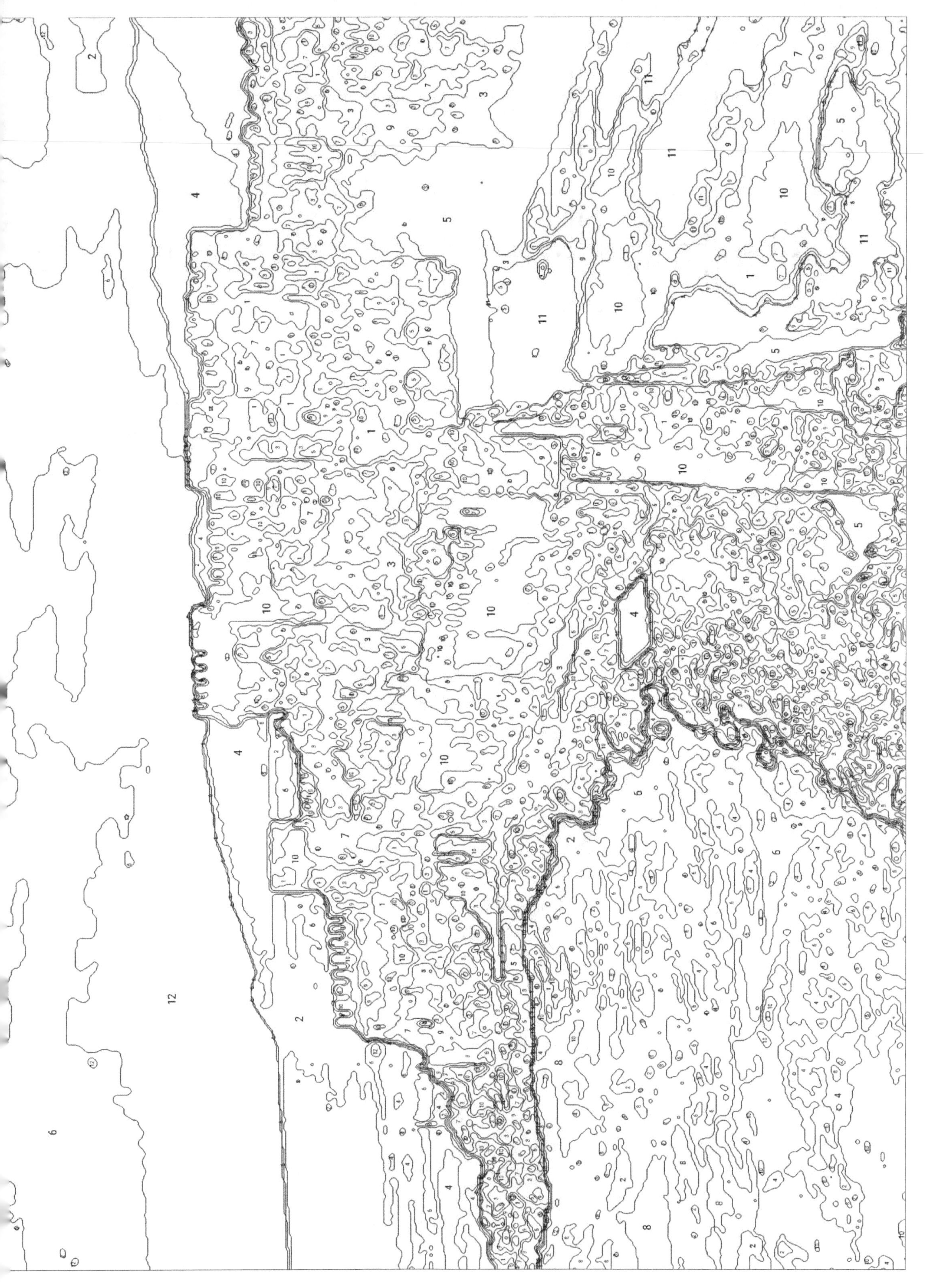

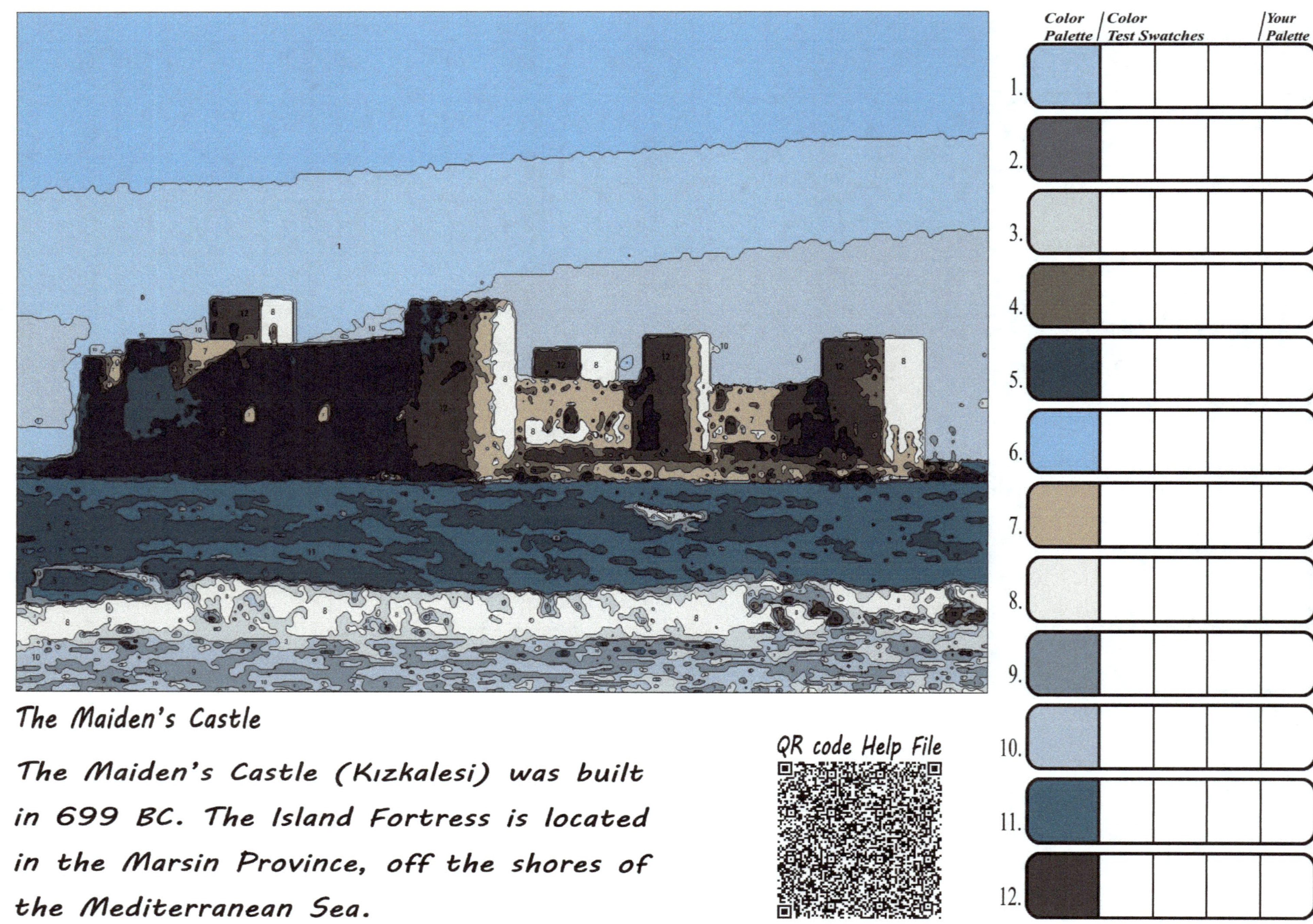

The Maiden's Castle

The Maiden's Castle (Kızkalesi) was built in 699 BC. The Island Fortress is located in the Marsin Province, off the shores of the Mediterranean Sea.

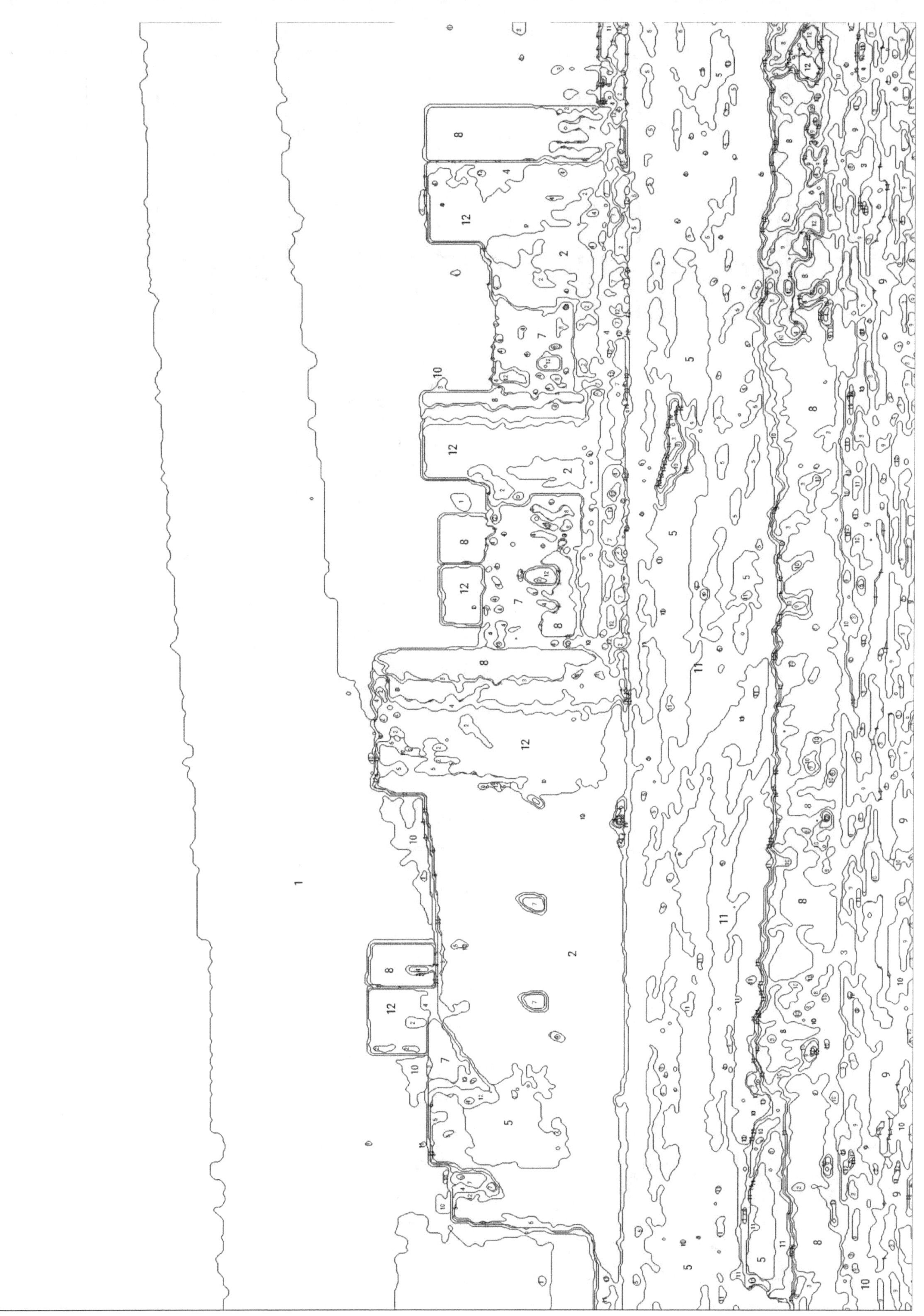

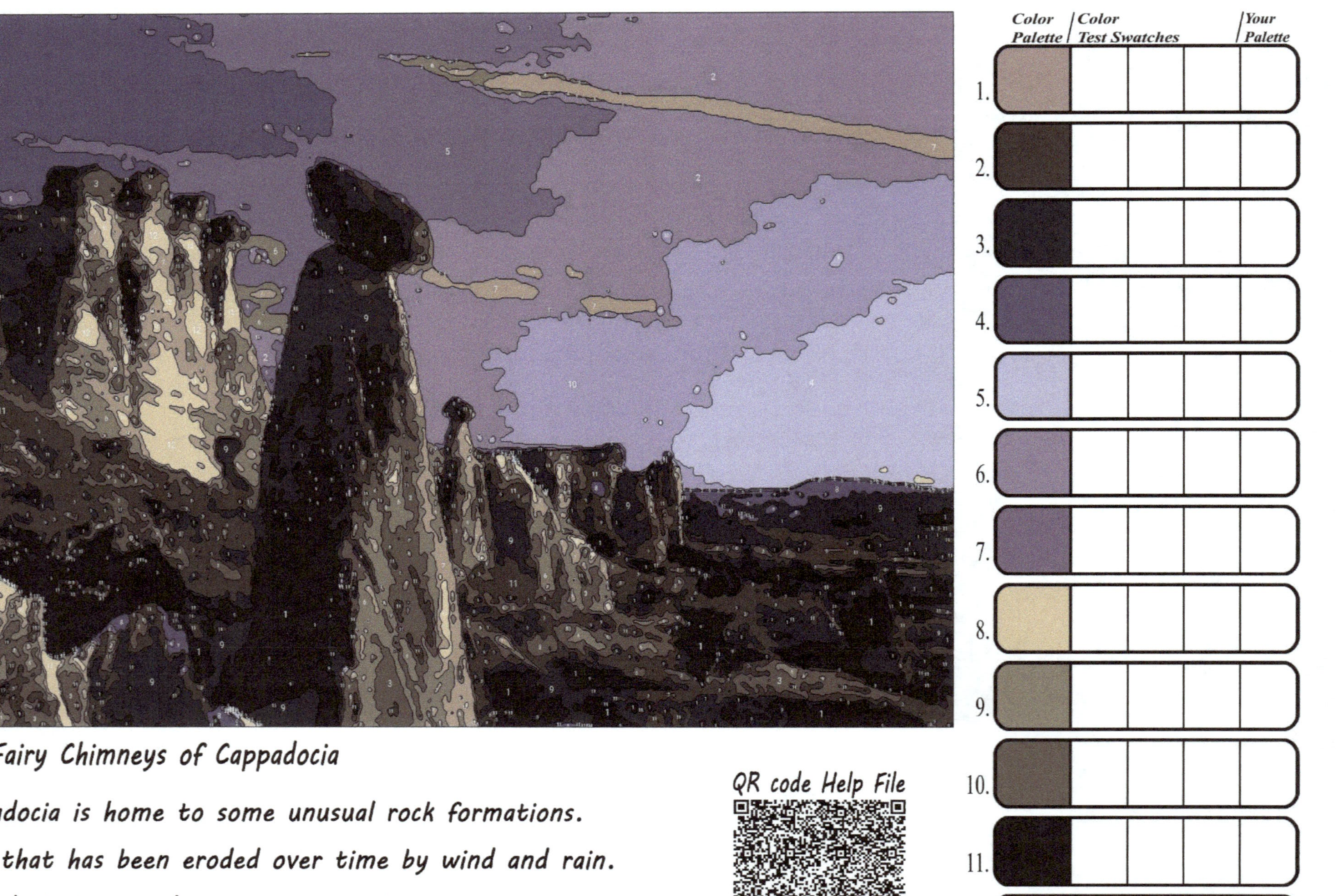

Color Palette	Color Test Swatches			Your Palette
1.				
2.				
3.				
4.				
5.				
6.				
7.				
8.				
9.				
10.				
11.				
12.				

The Fairy Chimneys of Cappadocia

Cappadocia is home to some unusual rock formations.

Rock that has been eroded over time by wind and rain.

Cappadocia is spread over seven provinces.

The largest province is Nevşehir.

QR code Help File

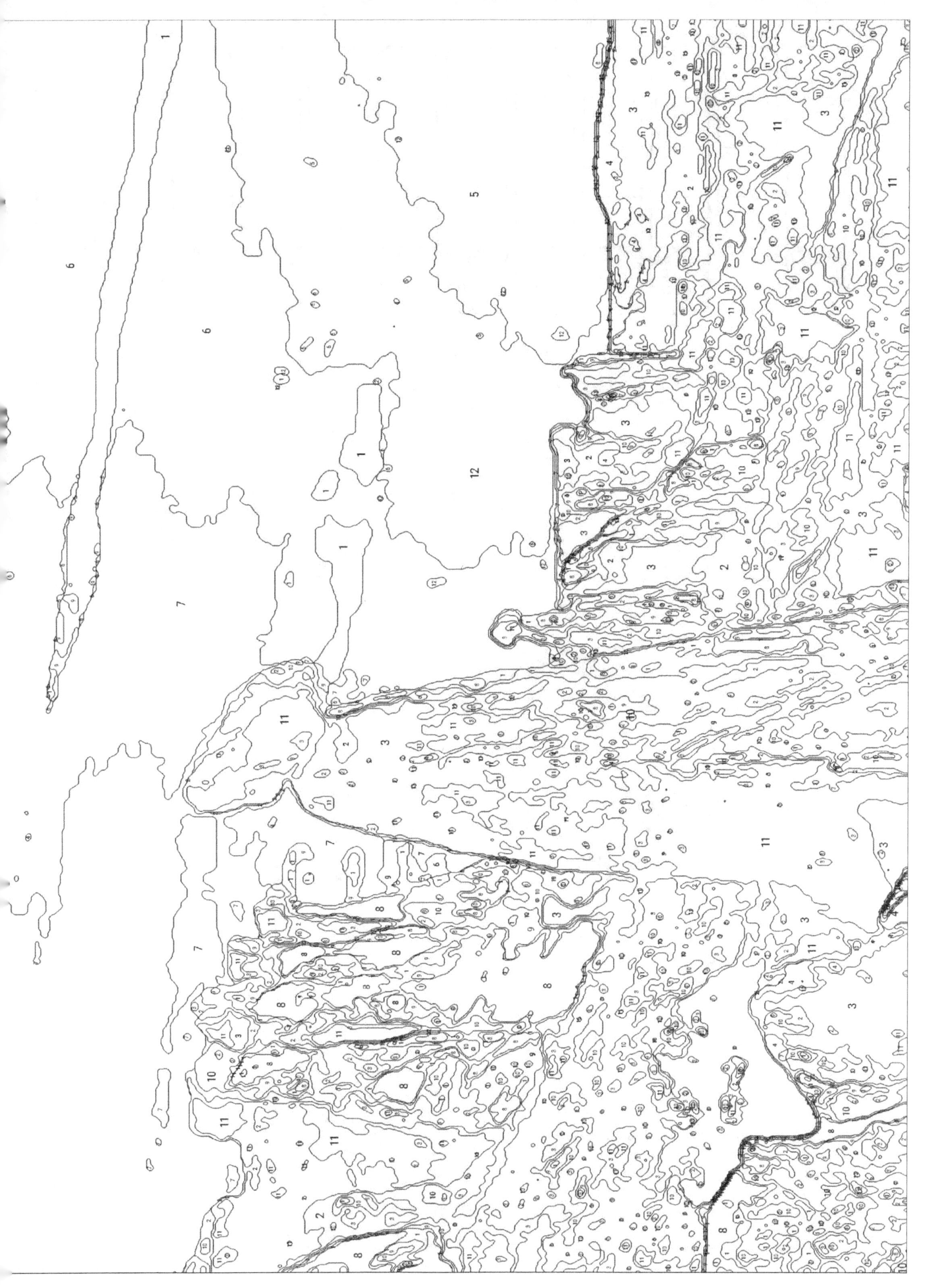

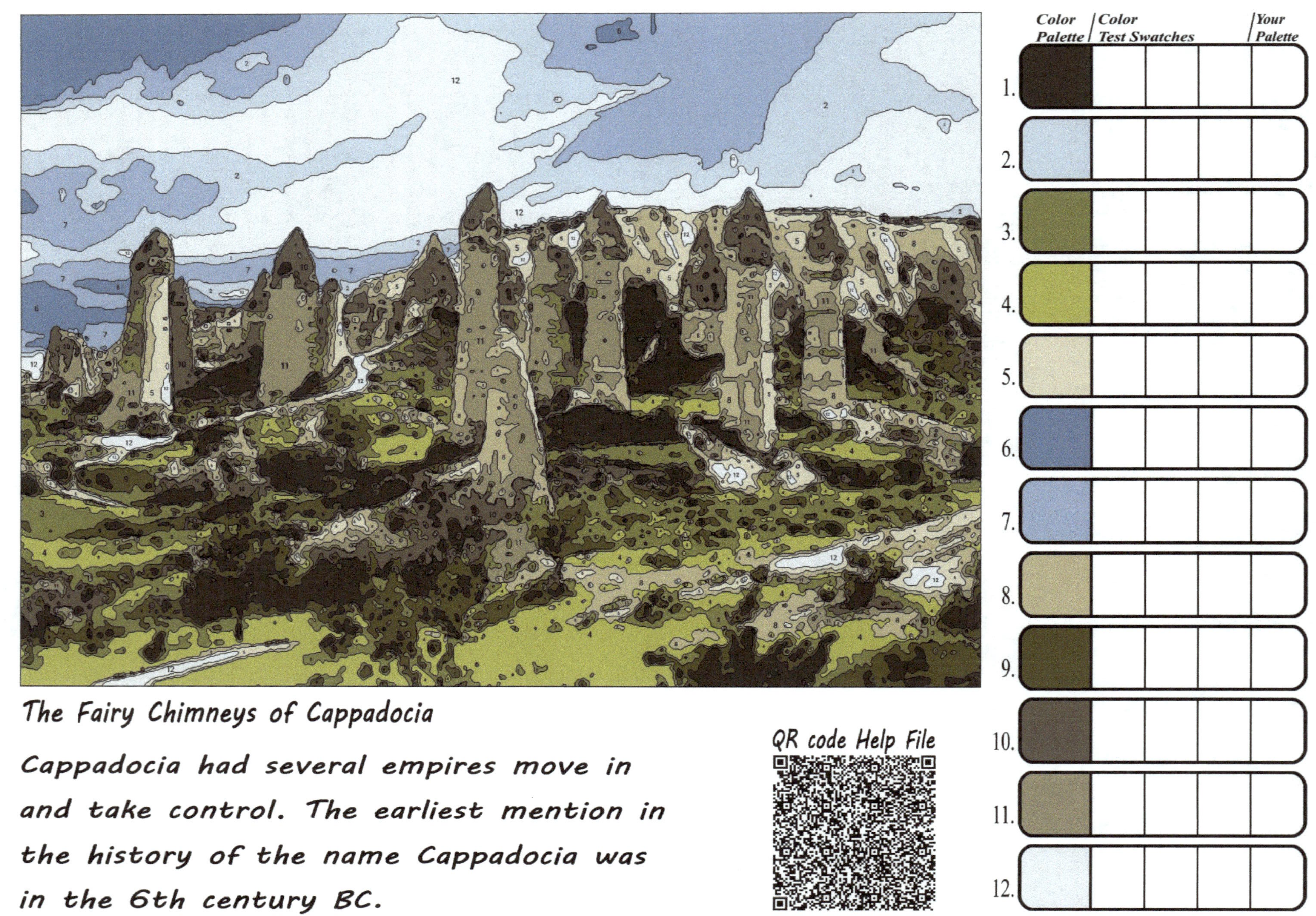

The Fairy Chimneys of Cappadocia

Cappadocia had several empires move in and take control. The earliest mention in the history of the name Cappadocia was in the 6th century BC.

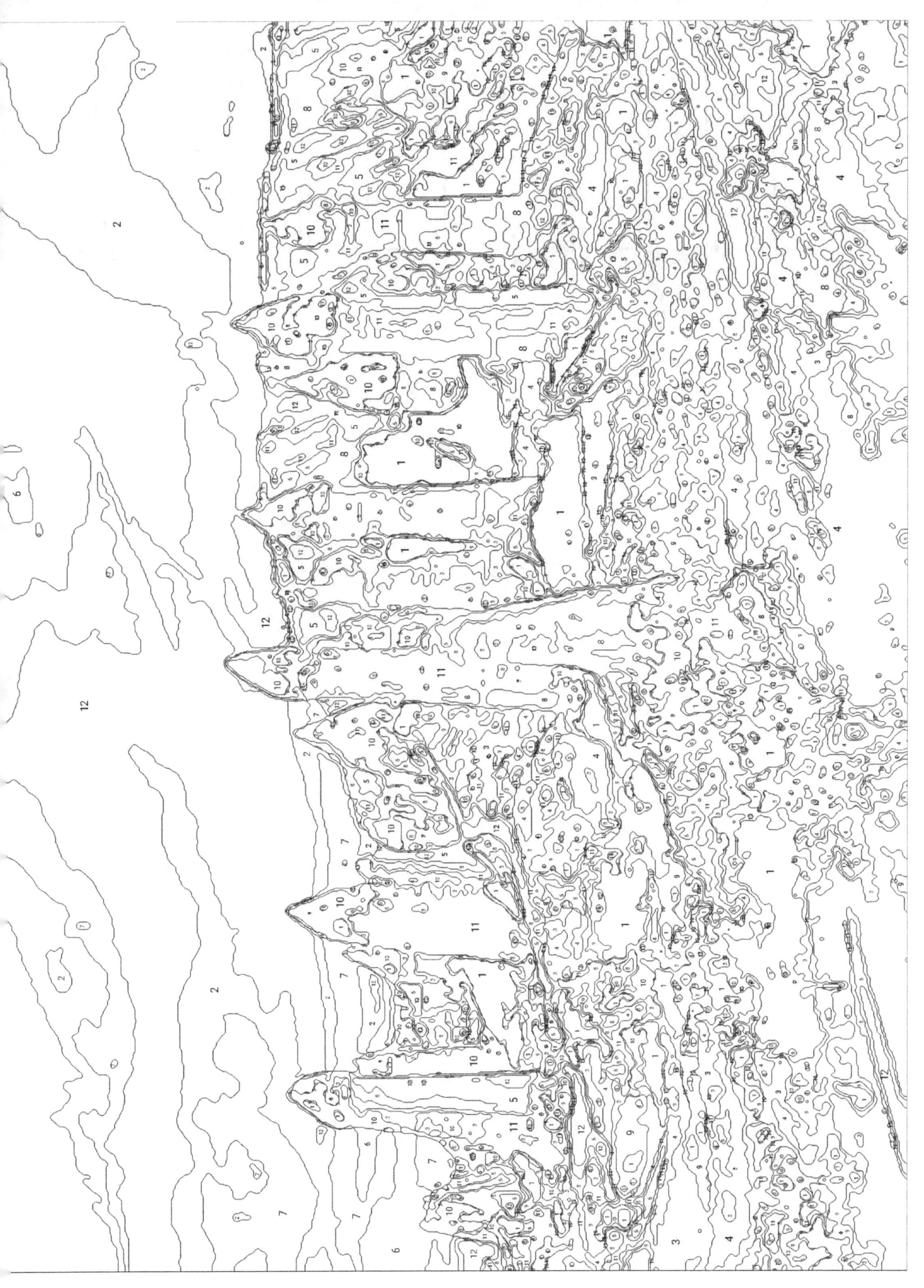

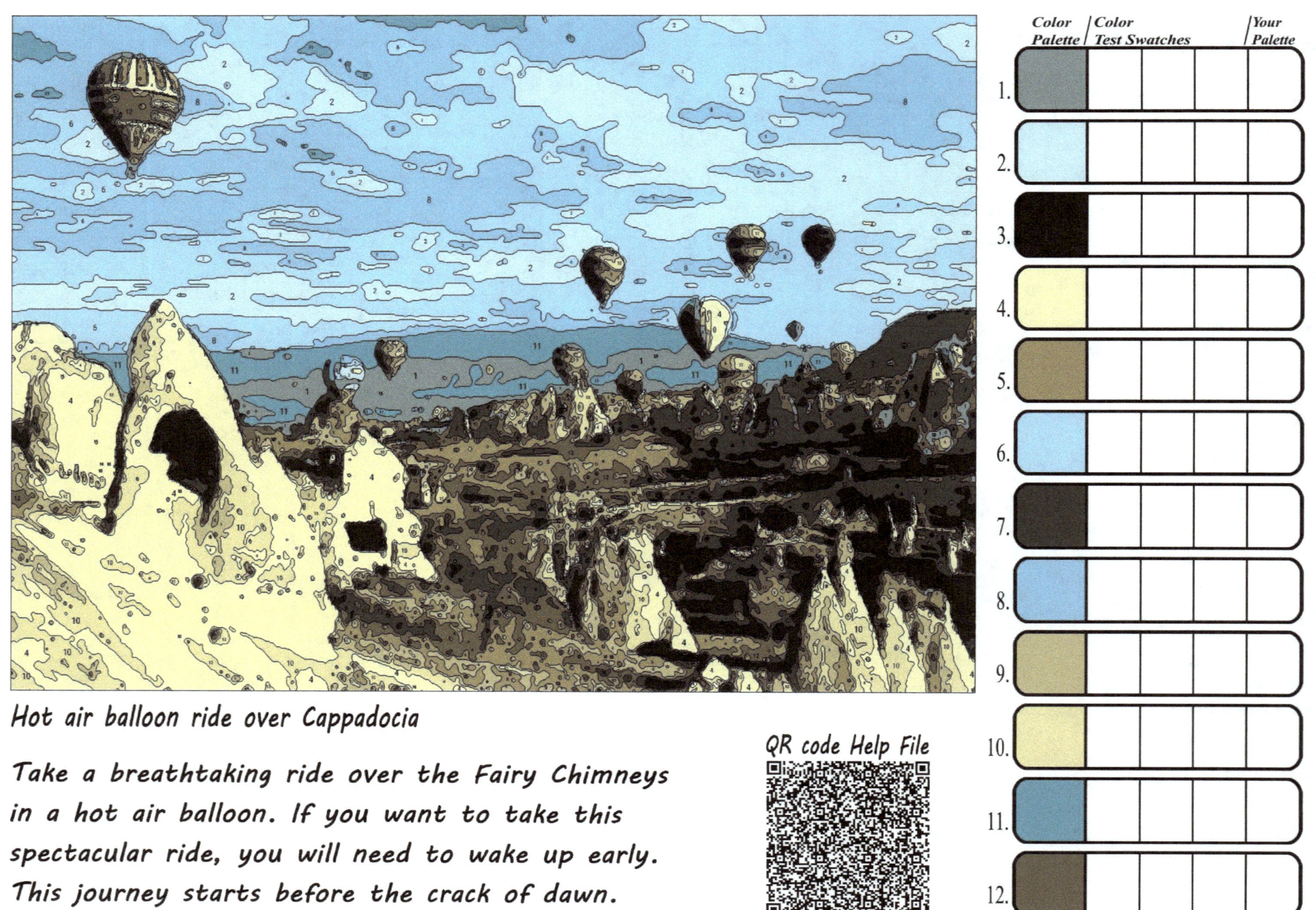

Hot air balloon ride over Cappadocia

Take a breathtaking ride over the Fairy Chimneys in a hot air balloon. If you want to take this spectacular ride, you will need to wake up early. This journey starts before the crack of dawn.

QR code Help File

	Color Palette	Color Test Swatches			Your Palette
1.					
2.					
3.					
4.					
5.					
6.					
7.					
8.					
9.					
10.					
11.					
12.					

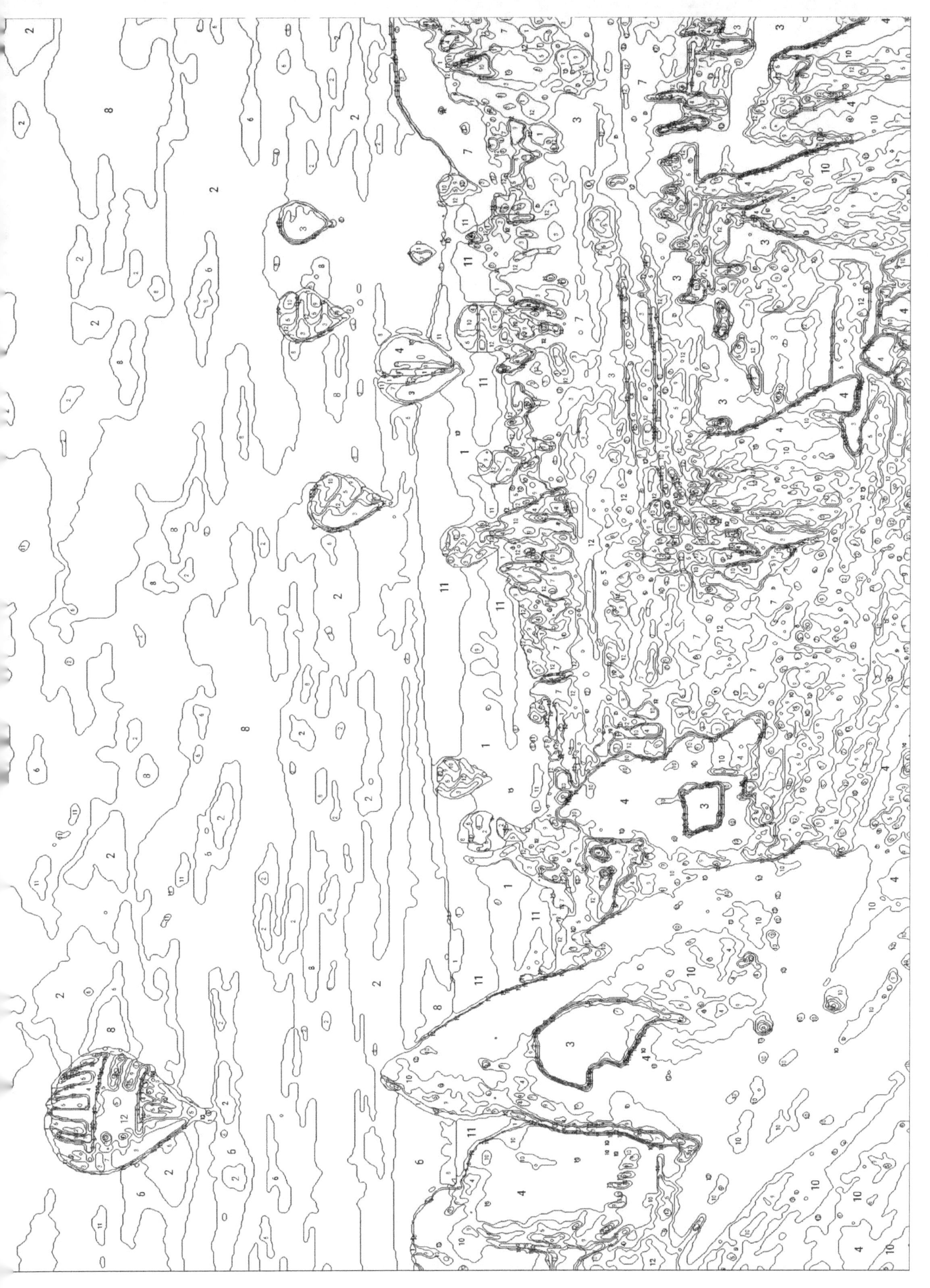

You have reached the end.
I hope you enjoyed your journey!
If you like this coloring book, keep
your eyes out for my next book. To keep
up to date on what's coming next, join me on
social media, visit my website, or Etsy shop.
I would like to take this time to thank
you for taking this journey
with me.

Thank you!

Connect with A Tailored Image at:

Facebook

Instagram

Youtube

Shop at:

Amazon

Etsy

Fineart America

Website

www.ingramcontent.com/pod-product-compliance
Lightning Source LLC
LaVergne TN
LVHW061253100826
845148LV00008B/1117

* 9 7 9 8 9 8 5 0 6 1 8 0 2 *